CW01095654

"If you obey all the rules, you miss all the fun."

Katherine Hepburn

Publisher: Edition Art, Design & Golf
                  Artigo GmbH
                  Im Leisibuehl 47
                  CH-8044 Zurich
                  Telephone: +41-79-400 97 43
                  Fax: +41-86079-400 97 43
                  Email: info@golfregeln.ch
                  www.golfregeln.ch

Text: Yves Cédric Ton-That, CH-8126 Zumikon

Illustrations: Roland Hausheer, CH-8049 Zurich
                  Yves Cédric Ton-That, CH-8126 Zumikon

Cover/layout: Arts & Media, CH-8049 Zurich

Photographs: Katharina Lütscher, CH-8005 Zurich
                  Tom Haller, CH-8008 Zurich

Translation: Louise Mawbey, D-86938 Schondorf am Ammersee
                  Yves Cédric Ton-That, CH-8126 Zumikon

Title of the original German version: "Soll ich droppen oder was...?"

Published 2002.

ISBN 3-9521596-4-6

Yves Cédric Ton-That

Should I Take a Drop or What...?

A Collection of Hilarious Stories about the Rules of Golf

1st Edition

Literature

This book is a summary of some of *The Rules of Golf* and *Decisions on the Rules of Golf* as interpreted by the author. It does not carry the official approval of the USGA, which does not therefore warrant the accuracy of the author's interpretations. *The Rules of Golf* which were effective as of January 1, 2000, remain current in the 2002-03 *Rules of Golf* book. The *Decisions on the Rules of Golf 2002-03* include changes to the *Decisions* as of 2002-03. *The Rules of Golf* and *Decisions on the Rules of Golf* will next be revised effective January 1, 2004. Readers should refer to the full text of the *Rules* and *Decisions* as published in the official publications, *The Rules of Golf* and *Decisions on the Rules of Golf,* which are published by the USGA/R&A.

Contents

Author

Yves Cédric Ton-That (born on December 20, 1972 in Switzerland) is an expert in the field of golf rules and etiquette. The handicap 5 player has many years' experience providing courses on the Rules of Golf and has acquired extensive knowledge of this subject in his capacity as captain. He is an official referee of the Swiss Golf Association and a lawyer.

Preface

Dear Golfer,

No other sport has as many rules as the game of golf – and no other sport's rules are so complicated! Therefore players can easily find themselves on sticky ground as far as the Rules are concerned, and because no one likes to admit their weaknesses, bizarre situations can arise. However, mastery of the Rules of Golf is a crucial requirement for an enjoyable round – after all they don't only consist of laws and prohibitions but also grant certain rights: they allow players to continue their game even if the ball has an unfortunate lie, for instance if it is stuck in a tree or comes to rest in a cowpat.

The following stories should enable you to refresh your knowledge of the basic rules in an entertaining and amusing way.

I hope you'll enjoy reading this book and I wish you many excellent days' golfing,

Yves Cédric Ton-That

PS: All the stories are almost totally imaginary. Any resemblance to existing persons is purely coincidental and of course absolutely unintentional...

The President's Cup

As I awoke that particular morning I didn't feel at all like getting up and even less like playing golf. My head was aching, my limbs felt extremely stiff and I wasn't at all looking forward to the coming day's golf. This irritated me a little, as this sense of anticipation was usually the best emotion of all – waking up with a tingling sensation all over my body and being desperate to get to the first tee. On the way to the golf course I would let my imagination run wild and picture a round where everything went right for once – everything, in one and the same round – and I'd be able to lower my handicap. My only other experience of this childlike sense of anticipation and impatience was from my childhood days. I would awake with similar emotions every Christmas morning and this had made growing up worthwhile, now every weekend was like Christmas. However I must admit that this comparison falls down in one very important respect – whereas I usually got what I'd wished for at Christmas, this has never been the case with golf. But this is what golf is all about; you learn how to come to terms with disappointment. Anyway, that's another story. As I arrived at the golf course the countryside was veiled in thick fog and you could sense that winter was in the air. My reluctance intensified. There was already a bustle of activity on the site – all kinds of people were scurrying backwards and forwards, trolleys were being pushed from one place to another and eager players were slaving away on the driving range. I fetched my scorecard from the pro shop where I was informed with great effusiveness that I had been assigned to His Excellency the Baron of Somewhere's group. I had been assigned to him, you notice, not the other way round. As I didn't seem to appreciate this generous gesture, and probably also because of my sceptical expression, the lady in the pro shop explained the situation in a slightly reproachful tone of voice. My aristocratic playing partner was the owner of Castle Something. Apparently he also owned the most famous and distinguished golf club in the area and was a personal guest of the president. "Oh," was all that I could think of to say in reply. I was still much too tired to get all excited about the apparent honor which had been bestowed on me. Nevertheless, I reasoned, if he owned his own golf course he must be able to play reasonably well and if not at least he'd know how to behave himself.

I got my things together and made my way to the tee. But when I arrived only the third member of the group and the starter were there, there was no sign of our aristocratic guest. There was still time though – almost a minute. But as the noble gentleman still hadn't turned up after the minute was up I wished my fellow-player a good game and started to tee-up my ball.

"You're only second on the list!" explained the starter. "I know," I replied, "but the first player hasn't arrived."

"Yes he has, I've already seen him."

"Yeah, but it's no use to us that he's somewhere on the site," I retorted, "we're playing a competition, our tee-off time has arrived and *life punishes those who come too late.*"

With these words of wisdom (which I had borrowed from Mikail Gorbachov who had used them on the occasion of the 40th anniversary of East Germany, just before the Berlin wall came down) I was referring to Rule 6-3 which states that anyone who doesn't start playing at the specified time will be disqualified.

Rule 6-3.a. Time of Starting
The player shall start at the time laid down by the Committee.

"We'll wait!" came the starter's stern reply.

He'd expressed himself so clearly that even I could understand what he was getting at – I assumed that this meant that our starting time had been officially postponed. And why should I get involved in a debate about it, after all it was only a paltry monthly Stableford competition, even though someone had decided to call it 'The President's Cup'. So I bent down, picked up my ball and my tee, and waited.

Soon afterwards I saw someone approaching the tee with measured steps. It had to be the Baron. He was pulling a trolley behind him on which there was a pink golf bag. And when I say pink, I mean pink. It wasn't burnt rose or salmon-colored – it was vivid pink. Since the section on etiquette doesn't mention anything specific about a color code on the golf course, I contented myself with a smirk. When he arrived at the tee he shook everyone's hand briefly and strongly, and muttered a sort of apology. Now that I could see his golf bag more closely I realised that it wasn't just that his bag was pink, it also boasted a glossy painted surface. No, no it wasn't what you're thinking. I admit that there could have been something in it but he immediately assured us that it was his wife's bag. In his rush that morning he'd put the wrong bag in the trunk. But it wasn't as bad as all that as they were his old clubs anyway.

So that's what he's like then, I thought to myself. I could just imagine him presenting his wife his old clubs in an act of unparalleled self-sacrifice, probably as a Christmas present. And this for one reason only – so that he finally had an excuse to buy himself some new ones. It had probably never even entered his head that his old cast-offs could be too heavy, too long, too old and too ugly for his wife. But fortunately I wasn't his wife and so I wasn't going to lose any sleep over it. He assured us that he could play with these clubs too.

After we had exchanged scorecards and the customary but meaningless pleasantries we were able to begin at last, albeit with a delay. The Lord of the Manor was to tee-off first, of course. He stepped onto the tee full of self-importance and proceeded to make a bizarre practice swing. I actually thought he was trying to be funny and, I have to admit, he was quite amusing, but then I realised that it had actually been his proper swing. To cut a long story short, his swing had very little to do with golf. At best you could catch butterflies with it, assuming you were holding a suitable net, but hit a golf ball...? It was now only too clear what was in store for the rest of the round. Have you any idea how arduous it is to play with someone like this? Every time he hits the ball – and I can assure you, he'll have to do this very often – you have to look away or you'll either feel queasy or by the end of the round you'll find yourself with exactly the same swing. So I knew I had to prepare myself to witness an extraordinary spectacle. But to my amazement he really did manage to hit the ball, and it even flew into the air. Not particularly far, not particularly high, but it left the ground, and at the end of the first hole he recorded a bogey. With his handicap stroke he had a net par for two Stableford points, which he was obviously very pleased with.

"It seems like you really can play with those old clubs," I remarked.

"Yes, yes," he acknowledged, but shortly afterwards admitted that they weren't all old ones after all. That morning, after he'd noticed his mishap, he'd gone to the Pro Shop and bought himself a new driver and a new putter. That aroused my suspicions and I counted his clubs – I had guessed correctly, there were 15. His standard set, or should I say his wife's, with 13 clubs, plus a new driver and a new putter made 15 in all.

"You've got one too many."

He then proceeded to count them for himself and also made it 15. After mulling it over for a short while he said, "But I'm only playing with 13 clubs. I've no intention of using my wife's driver and putter so there's absolutely no problem." His argument sounded convincing, but nevertheless the maximum number of clubs stated in Rule 4-4. refers to the clubs a player *is carrying* when he starts his round, not to those he actually uses.

Rule 4-4.a. Selection and Addition of Clubs

The player shall start a stipulated round with not more than fourteen clubs. [...]

After I had explained the rule to him I concluded by commenting that he would have to deduct two points from his total.

Rule 32-1.b. Stableford Competitions

[...]

Note 1: Maximum of 14 clubs (Rule 4-4) – Penalties applied as follows: From total points scored for the round, deduction of two points for each hole at which any breach occurred; maximum deduction per round: four points.

That hit him where it hurt. He just couldn't believe that the two points which he had worked so hard to win were going to be taken away from him.

"We'll see about that young man," he fumed, brandishing his wife's putter at me with a bright red face. "Which one's too many? This one? This is the one, isn't it?"

But before I had the chance to reply he'd already bent the club out of all recognition and flung it into the bin, thereby destroying both the club and the atmosphere in one go – and this was only the first hole!

My newfound friend's next drive was as poor as might be expected. The ball disappeared off to the right into a large bush – it was clearly a lost cause. As he returned to his trolley I assumed he was going to fetch a new ball and make a provisional shot, but he just threw his club into the bag and marched off. He obviously fully expected to be able to find the ball. He must have been shortsighted, what a handicap that must be!

When we reached the bushes we started to look for the ball.

"Keep on looking you two, but over in that direction a bit," he ordered after a while, pointing to a particularly dense patch, "I'll just go back and hit a provisional ball!"

I'd never heard anything like it in my life, on top of everything else he was clearly too lazy to look for his own ball.

"I'm sorry," I eventually replied, "but you can't do that." His eyes started to flash in anger and I was worried that he was going to use his new driver to club me to death.

"Why on earth not?" he asked.

I regretted having brought it up in the first place and was now forced to explain Rule 27-2 in more detail. "You should have thought about it earlier as a provisional ball can only be played *before* the player sets off to look for the first one. If you go back now and play a ball it will automatically be classed as a new ball and will become the ball in play under penalty of one stroke."

Rule 27-2. Provisional Ball
a. Procedure

[...] The player shall inform his opponent in match play or his marker or a fellow-competitor in stroke play that he intends to play a provisional ball, and he shall play it before he or his partner goes forward to search for the original ball.

If he fails to do so and plays another ball, such ball is not a provisional ball and becomes the ball in play under penalty of stroke and distance (Rule 27-1); the original ball is deemed to be lost.

"Of course, you could carry on looking until the five minutes are up and play the original ball if we do happen to find it."

He was now totally confused and the anger in his eyes subsided. Obviously it hadn't dawned on him before that golf could be so complicated, and he suddenly sank to the ground in despair. I can only assume that on his estate golf is played in accordance with the Lord of the Manor's own rules.

The Baron turned his back on us and disappeared into the bushes with a hangdog expression to continue the search.

"I've got it," he suddenly announced, in a somewhat subdued tone.

Shortly afterwards we heard a dull thud, and the earth shook – he must have hit the ground. The continual snapping of branches, coupled with the other noises, signified no good. He eventually came crawling out of the bushes with his ball in his hand. His hair was dishevelled and covered with leaves and other 'loose impediments'. He'd obviously forced his ball so deep into the bushes that there was absolutely no chance of getting it out again. With beads of sweat on his forehead and a trembling voice he turned to me questioningly, "I declare the ball unplayable and I'm going back to the tee."

"I'm sorry..." I began again, but before I could finish the sentence he interrupted me with the words, "Yeah, yeah, I expected you to say something like that."

I really did feel sorry for him but what could I do? After all, I wasn't the one who invented Rule 28. This does allow a player to declare his ball unplayable and take a drop under penalty of one stroke, however not on the previous tee, but on the spot where the *previous shot* had been made. Of course it's perfectly possible that this spot is indeed the previous tee, but the Baron had taken a whole series of strokes in the bushes in the meantime, so the spot where his last shot had been made was now obviously somewhere in the bushes. Nevertheless Rule 28 does allow the ball to be dropped at two other places as well, and these were much better options for the Baron anyway.

Rule 28. Ball Unplayable

[...]

If the player deems his ball to be unplayable, he shall, under penalty of one stroke:

a. Play a ball as nearly as possible at the spot from which the original ball was last played (see Rule 20-5); or

b. Drop a ball within two club-lengths of the spot where the ball lay, but not nearer the hole; or

c. Drop a ball behind the point where the ball lay, keeping that point directly between the hole and the spot on which the ball is dropped, with no limit to how far behind that point the ball may be dropped. [...]

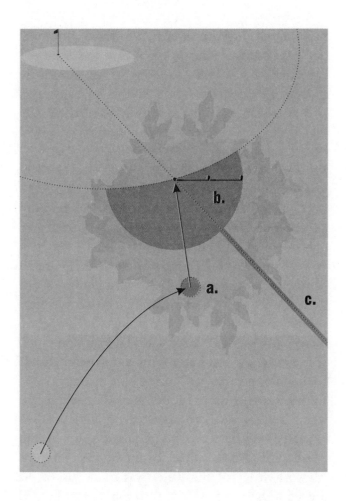

There are three options available to a player to take a drop if he declares his ball unplayable. Each carries a penalty of one stroke.

But I didn't draw his attention to these additional options as we were playing Stableford and as far as I could tell he had taken so many strokes already he couldn't get any more points on this hole anyway.

"I'll just drop one up the fairway somewhere," he said coolly and added, "just for fun, of course, it won't count."

Just for fun eh? I was pleased to hear that he'd not lost his ability to have fun as well as his ball, and I kept quiet. Of course in Stableford when you can't get any more points it isn't exactly good manners to play on, but I let it go.

It went on like this for the whole 18 holes and I believe we all three played the worst round of our lives. But when we'd finished my fellow-competitor still refused to deduct the two points for having too many clubs on the 1st hole. He'd taken it upon himself to erase the deduction on his own scorecard so I refused to give my signature as his marker.

In the changing room I found out what he'd meant when he said we'd see about that. The president appeared with the scorecard in question, armed with a ballpoint pen and subjected me to a long lecture. My knowledge of the Rules was of no use as he argued with such presidential reasoning that I ended up signing. But the real reason why I signed was not his powers of persuasion but because I'd had time to calculate the Baron's points. He'd got so few that

I thought it advisable to back down – he would then be second from last. The last position was taken up by my humble self as I later disqualified myself for knowingly signing an incorrect scorecard.

Should I Take a Drop or What...?

E ver since I've been able to play golf I've taken part in the annual Swiss championship, and as far as I can remember it hasn't just rained throughout every competition, it has bucketed down. Playing under such unpleasant conditions is always extremely challenging as the round is beset with all sorts of difficulties which actually have nothing at all to do with golf. Hitting the ball becomes secondary and you have to get it around the course as best you can. After all this, the real winner is the player who manages to keep his belongings dry. Last time, to everyone's amazement, the weather was lovely – I took part anyway.

The first round went quite well. After all I had given it my best, as I always do on the first day of tournaments played over a number of days, because the first round has a decisive effect on the next day's starting time – the worst players start first, the best last. So on the first day I fight tooth and nail, even if all seems lost. Just one shot difference could mean an entire hour longer in bed. (I had learned my lesson the hard way. I once took it easy in a championship and the next day I was due to tee off first with a starting time of 5.30 in the morning. In the end we teed-off a bit later anyway as we had to wait until it got light – but that's another story.)

So I returned to the scene of the battle around lunchtime the following day and was soon on my way to the first tee. My fellow-competitors were already there. We introduced ourselves and exchanged score-cards. The player whose scorecard I was to mark had the honor. I'll call him D. to avoid any embarrass-ment.

"I'm going to play a Top-Flite," muttered D. as he began to tee-up.

It would have been more accurate to say "I'm going to play a slice," as his ball flew in a gigantic curve straight into a nearby river. This in itself was no-thing extraordinary as the first tee shot on this golf course is tailor-made for just this type of shot. There are said to be people who, after a few failed attempts, have thrown in the towel at this point to seek solace in the bar for the rest of the day. D's second attempt was the spitting image of his first until the ball sud-denly got caught in a tree and plunged down the embankment. D. made threatening gestures in the direction of the embankment and ran off, waving his arms wildly. I couldn't understand what he was getting so wound up about – as far as I could tell he'd had a lucky break.

D. was now standing on top of the embankment and he cautiously tried to climb down the other side to the river. But almost as soon as he had set foot on the wet slope he disappeared from sight and a loud crash could be heard. He must have flown down the embankment at great speed, as when I reached him he was cursing as he plucked leaves and various small animals out of his hair, his clothes covered in dirt. I didn't say a word.

But what was to follow totally dumbfounded me. D. had his ball in his hand and was placing it with meticulous care on a patch of grass on the embankment. I was lost for words and asked myself what on earth he could be doing. However I didn't get the chance to ask him about it as by the time I'd found my voice again he'd already addressed the ball. So I just assumed that the ball had moved as a result of the fall and D. had replaced it in accordance with the Rules – incurring a penalty stroke, of course.

Rule 18. Ball at Rest Moved
18-2. By Player, Partner, Caddie or Equipment
a. General

When a player's ball is in play, if:

(i) the player, his partner or either of their caddies lifts or moves it, touches it purposely [...] or causes it to move [...]

(ii) equipment of the player or his partner causes the ball to move, the player shall incur a penalty stroke. The ball shall be replaced [...]

D. took a swing and hacked the ball tolerably well off the embankment so that it now lay in the middle of the fairway. I counted again: 1 – tee shot into the water, 2 – penalty stroke, 3 – tee shot onto the embankment, 4 – replacement with penalty stroke, 5 – onto the fairway.

"So, you've taken 5 up till now," I declared, interested to see if D. would agree.

"Whaat?" he cried indignantly and immediately corrected me, "no, 3."

This must have been unintentional, I reasoned – having taken as many shots as this it would be easy to forget one here and there – so I counted out his strokes for him.

"Alright then, 4," he suggested.

It was just like being at an oriental bazaar. After I had made it clear that I had not gone there to barter he said, "The ball didn't move at all, I just identified it and replaced it. There's no penalty for that and so I have only taken 4 after all." He looked at me triumphantly with a roguish grin on his face.

"Oh, I see, it didn't move," I repeated, "if that's the case I'm sorry about the mistake – obviously a penalty stroke in accordance with Rule 18 won't apply."

He must have found great satisfaction in this as, despite his terrible start, a satisfied smile lit up his face until I remarked casually, "Instead you've incurred a penalty stroke because you lifted your ball to identify it without informing one of us first."

Rule 12-2. Identifying Ball

[...]

Before lifting the ball, the player must announce his intention to his opponent in match play or his marker or a fellow-competitor in stroke play and mark the position of the ball. He must then give his opponent, marker or fellow-competitor an opportunity to observe the lifting and replacement. If he lifts his ball without announcing his intention in advance, marking the position of the ball or giving his opponent, marker or fellow-competitor an opportunity to observe, or if he lifts his ball for identification in a hazard, or cleans it more than necessary for identification, he shall incur a penalty of one stroke and the ball shall be replaced.

[...]

His jaw dropped and he stared at me in disbelief, he then went extremely pale and started to gasp for breath. I thought it was better to beat a tactful retreat as I assumed he would want to come to terms with his anger and sorrow alone. We finished the hole in silence and after D. had finally managed to persuade the ball into the hole with his fifth putt I recorded a 12 for him. It had all been my fault.

The hours that followed were absurd as before every single shot D. asked me whether he was allowed to do what he was planning to do, and even after I had assented, he double-checked it with, "Are you absolutely positive?"

After about 12 holes he eventually began to play his own game again. It was just at this moment that he put his ball next to a fir tree which was supported by a taut wire rope. The ball lay in such a dreadful position that he could only swing back about 10 inches before his club got tangled up in the wire. I was convinced that with a swing as short as this D. would never manage the 150 yards to the green. But because he was getting ready to play the ball from this position anyway I asked him what he was doing.

He interrupted me brusquely, "I'm trying to play golf!" That's what he'd been trying to do for the last 3 hours – but I didn't want to go into that.

"This is an immovable obstruction, you can take free relief."

He glanced at me sceptically. He just couldn't grasp the idea that I suddenly wanted to help him – I was one of the bad guys.

"But it says in the Local Rules on the scorecard that only staked trees are considered to be immovable obstructions. But this is a *wire rope!*" he rejoined.

"That's right," I explained further, "and it means that in our case the *entire tree together with the wire rope* is *not* classed as an immovable obstruction. However the wire rope *in itself* is, and always will be, artificial, and is therefore an immovable obstruction. If this type of object interferes with a player's stance or, as here, his swing, he can have free relief and take a drop."

Top: Local Rules often grant relief from staked trees in accordance with the procedure for immovable obstructions. This refers to the tree and the stakes as a single entity.

Below: Even if nothing is mentioned in the Local Rules the stakes themselves, as well as stabilising wire ropes, are artificial objects in their own right and are therefore always deemed to be obstructions.

Definition "Obstructions"

An "obstruction" is anything artificial [...]

Rule 24-2. Immovable Obstruction

a. Interference

Interference by an immovable obstruction occurs when a ball lies in or on the obstruction, or so close to the obstruction that the obstruction interferes with the player's stance or the area of his intended swing. [...]

D. looked at me with a bemused expression. My endless jabbering on about the Rules had been too much for him and he had evidently been unable to follow me. Totally bewildered he asked, "Should I take a drop then or what?"

"Of course," I answered, "within one club-length of the nearest point where you can stand and take a swing without being obstructed by the wire rope."

Rule 24-2. Immovable Obstruction

b. Relief

[...]

(i) Through the Green: If the ball lies through the green, the nearest point of relief shall be determined which is not in a hazard or on a putting green. The player shall lift the ball and drop it within one club-length of and not nearer the hole than the nearest point of relief on a part of the course which avoids interference (as defined) by the immovable obstruction and is not in a hazard or on a putting green.

He asked me to show him the exact spot where he could take a drop, and before he dropped his ball he double-checked yet again, "You're absolutely positive about this, aren't you?" I was absolutely positive about one thing – it could have been worse. After all, it hadn't rained.

The Ball
in a Cowpat

Recently I went to Zumikon to play golf. But not at the Zumikon Golf Club as you would expect, but at the 'Zurich Golf & Country Club', for this is what this exclusive club is called, despite the fact that Zurich can't be seen from up there – not even on a clear day. O.K. then, there is a precedent for this; my home club is called Rheinblick (Rhine View) and as long as I've been playing there I've never once seen the River Rhine. Even when it burst its banks. You are probably thinking that these are two exceptional cases – not by a long shot, in Switzerland we have many such examples. The Montreux Golf Club is situated a great distance away from Montreux in Aigle, and if you take the Bubikon exit when driving to the Bubikon Golf Club you'll have a long search ahead of you. There are other examples like this but I can't describe them in detail here because I never have managed to find the clubs in question.

The interesting thing about this is that these names were not chosen at random. They were also not selected to suit a particular marketing strategy – the reason is purely tactical. The journey is aimed at fraying the visiting players' nerves to such an extent that, if they ever do manage to find the golf course, their vexation and desperation means that they have to write off the first few holes at least. Home advantage is alive and kicking!

In Zumikon I don't have to face this problem because I live there and over time I've come to know the way. If there's no traffic the journey from my house to the golf club takes 28 seconds. (However car journeys this short are bad for the engine so I chose a club which is a bit further away.)

I arrived in plenty of time to find out about the form of play. It was going to be a Greensomes tournament, but this didn't tell me much. The lady in the pro shop enlightened me.

"You play in a team of two. Both players tee off, you choose the best drive and then alternate strokes until the ball is holed."

I then realised why it said in the invitation that married couples shouldn't play together – it would be better to play with another couple. The two ladies together and the two men together. This problem didn't apply to me because I always play with my golfing pal Max. But our fellow-competitors were a married couple after all. We couldn't wait!

The first tee at Zumikon is fantastic. An enormous fir tree to the right and another to the left, which isn't a problem of course if you hit the ball straight. But who on earth manages to play the first shot straight? Our fellow-competitor's tee shot was a quick hook which was all the more remarkable because he also topped it. To put it in a nutshell, the ball flew low over the ladies tee and disappeared to the left under the fir tree. I'd always thought that this fir tree was only a problem for left-handed players, but now I know better.

His wife shot him a reproachful look. "What did you do that for?"

"What do you mean by that? You don't imagine I did it on purpose, do you?!" he replied angrily.

"You could at least be embarrassed about it!" she shouted and marched off to the ladies tee. As she teed-up she announced scornfully, "We'll take my drive," but then proceeded to pull her drive to the left as well – inducing an exultant "Great shot!" from her husband.

But the best was yet to come as when we reached the ball it was actually lying in the rough, in the middle of a cowpat. I'll spare you a detailed description – suffice it to say it wasn't exactly the most pleasant of positions.

"We'll take relief," the man stated, as it was now his turn.

"What from?" I asked in astonishment.

"You know, from the cowpat," he replied at once.

I asked him to show me the passage in the rulebook where taking relief from a cowpat was provided for and he mumbled something about animal tracks.

"Correct me if I'm wrong, but as far as I'm aware cows are neither burrowing animals, nor reptiles and they're not exactly famous for their flying skills either."

Definition „Abnormal Ground Conditions"
An "abnormal ground condition" is any casual water, ground under repair, or hole, cast or runway on the course made by a burrowing animal, a reptile or a bird.

"Alright, alright, then it must be a loose impediment because it's a natural object," he replied impatiently. "It certainly is natural but I wouldn't exactly call it loose. Besides, since it's adhering to the ball you're not allowed to remove it."

"Now you listen up," he replied, obviously annoyed,
"it's common sense to be given free relief for this."
It was a nice argument, but after many years studying
the Rules of Golf I've reached the conclusion that
they have absolutely nothing at all to do with common sense. I explained this to him and once again
asked him to show me the exact passage in the rulebook.

Eventually he asked challengingly, "What would you
suggest then, Mr. Know-it-All?"

"Well," I replied after a moment's consideration, "the
basic principle of the game of golf is that the ball
should be played where it lies..."

His eyes widened almost to the size of the golf ball
itself at the thought, but there was apparently no

way out. Suddenly, he picked up his club, lent over the ball, took a long swing - and missed the ball completely.

"Oops, missed!" he said and then added with a smirk, "your turn, darling."

She was seething with rage and uttered things which I wouldn't like to repeat in polite company, and as it seemed like she was about to completely blow a fuse I stepped in with the words, "You missed the ball deliberately to avoid playing the shot. That's against the Rules!"

Decision 29-1/7 Player Misses Ball Purposely So Partner Would Play Ball Over Water

Q. A and B, partners in a foursome competition, were faced with a difficult shot over a pond. A, a poor player, swung but purposely missed the ball. B, an expert player, then played the ball to the green. Is this permissible?

A. No. Since A had no intention of moving the ball, he did not play a stroke — see Definition of "Stroke" — and it remained his turn to play [...]

"Your feigned stroke doesn't count. It's still your turn, otherwise you'll incur two penalty strokes."

Rule 29. Threesomes and Foursomes
29-3. Stroke Play

If the partners play a stroke or strokes in incorrect order, such stroke or strokes shall be cancelled and the side shall incur a penalty of two strokes.The side shall correct the error by playing a ball in correct order as nearly as possible at the spot from which it first played in incorrect order.

[...]

"Now listen here, I didn't miss on purpose. I tried to hit the ball off the top because it was in the cowpat. It's not as easy as you think, you're welcome to try it, if you want."

I declined. So no penalty was given and it was his wife's turn.

Decision 29-1/6 Player Misses Ball Accidentally When Making Stroke

Q. In a foursome event, A and B are partners. A attempts to strike the ball and misses. Whose turn is it to play?

A. An accidental miss is a stroke — see Definition of "Stroke." It is B's turn to play.

To my amazement she had calmed herself down. She coolly fished a ball out of her bag, measured out two club-lengths and calmly announced, "I declare the ball unplayable." She then dropped the ball.

"You're not allowed to use a new ball," chipped in her husband, "you've got to drop the original ball." He pointed to the cowpat, "That one, there." He was giving me the impression that he really liked his wife.

"Then be a love and fetch it for me," she replied, "and please don't forget to clean it."

Before they had the chance to continue their quarrel, I made it clear to them that they could leave the ball where it was and drop a new ball without a second thought, as Rule 28 doesn't say drop *the* ball, but drop *a* ball, and therefore a different ball can be used.

Rule 28. Ball Unplayable

[...]

If the player deems his ball to be unplayable, he shall, under penalty of one stroke:

[...]

b. Drop a ball [...]

The round was to continue exactly as it had begun – he hid his ball in the bushes, she hacked it out into the water and they plugged the ball for each other in the bunkers. I was glad I wasn't married.

PS: On certain courses in the Swiss Alps Local Rules have been made which grant free relief from *fresh* cowpats. However if the ball happens to lie on a *dry* cowpat it must be played where it lies. But they forgot one thing – a cowpat which is dry on the outside could still be moist on the inside...

Golf Rules Best
Before 12/31/2003

It was my first tournament in the new year and I was filled with childlike excitement. At long last I could indulge in my favorite sport again. Of course I had played two rounds as soon as the last remains of snow had melted from the course, but nevertheless the first official tournament in the new year had something special about it – it was to be played in accordance with the revised Rules which had come into effect on 1/1/2000. I almost felt a little nervous.

As I arrived at the first tee I greeted my fellow-competitors. "Yves Ton-That," I said amicably.

"I know who you are," replied my fellow-competitor brusquely.

There was something in his voice that I couldn't quite put my finger on, but one thing was for sure, it wasn't enthusiasm. He then growled out his own name, "Gardener," and shook my hand reluctantly.

I was somewhat taken aback, but just at this moment the other fellow-competitor stepped forward.

"My name's Tom," he announced, with a beam on his face and a firm handshake.

"Yves," I replied, "pleased to meet you."

And I really was pleased – I knew straight away that we would get along swimmingly and have a superb round of golf. Therefore I resolved not to let the round be spoiled by the other killjoy.

But he chipped in again. "Just don't you think that you've got to explain the Rules to me. I'm well prepared."

"Super," I replied, as I appreciate it greatly when my fellow-competitors know the Rules and I can keep my mouth shut. After all, there's nothing worse than having to explain a rule to a fellow-competitor, or pointing out to him that he's landed himself a string of penalty strokes. This is always a very tricky matter. Suddenly Gardener reached into his golf bag and pulled out a whole chain of rulebooks which he held up, right in front of my nose.

"You see, I've got everything we need."

"You haven't got my book," I answered, without a modicum of modesty.

His reaction to this comment was to pull a face which left me in no doubt as to what he thought of my work – absolutely nothing. I therefore thought it prudent to make no further remarks, despite the fact that I would have had great pleasure in pointing out to him that all his books were out of date, as the Rules had been revised on 1st January, just as they are every four years. I didn't say a word. Perhaps a more suitable opportunity for pointing this out would arise later...

This point arrived at the second hole. My ball lay in the bunker next to a puddle.

"I'll take relief here as the puddle would interfere with my stance," I announced.

Definition "Casual Water"

"Casual water" is any temporary accumulation of water [...] which is visible [...]

Definition "Abnormal Ground Conditions"

An "abnormal ground condition" is any casual water [...]

Rule 25-1. Abnormal Ground Condition
a. Interference

Interference by an abnormal ground condition occurs when a ball lies in or touches the condition or when such a condition interferes with the player's stance or the area of his intended swing.
[...]

"O.K.," came the reply.

I determined the nearest point at which I could take my stance without being obstructed by the puddle and where the ball itself wouldn't be in the water either. I then marked the spot with a tee and measured out a club-length.

"Would you kindly tell me what on earth you're up to?" asked Gardener, indignantly.

I shrugged my shoulders. "I'm taking relief..."

"Sorry, rules expert," he butted in, "I really don't want to have to teach you the Rules, but why on earth are you measuring out a club-length in the bunker?"

I had no idea of the misery that was in store for me. After clearing my throat I attempted to explain, "Rule

25..." – but I'd hardly even started the sentence before he interrupted again.

"No, no, you've got no idea!" he shouted, pouncing on his golf bag like a predatory animal.

He dragged out a rulebook once more and quoted Rule 25-1.b. at full length – well, the old version anyway. According to this the ball had to be dropped at the nearest point of relief in the bunker – at exactly this point, not within a club-length. However in order to simplify Rule 25 a club-length had been introduced in the new version for relief in a bunker as well.

Rule 25-1. Abnormal Ground Condition
b. Relief

[...]

(i) Through the Green: [...] The player shall lift the ball and drop it without penalty within one club-length of and not nearer the hole than the nearest point of relief, on a part of the course [...]

(ii) In a Bunker: If the ball is in a bunker, the player shall lift and drop the ball either:

(a) Without penalty, in accordance with Clause (i) above, except that the nearest point of relief must be in the bunker and the ball must be dropped in the bunker [...]

I tried again. "But Rule 25..." I wanted to draw his attention to the revision but sadly without success. He interrupted yet again. "The Rules are obviously not your particular strong point," he said mockingly.

The situation went from bad to worse. In the meantime I wrangled with my conscience. If I drew his attention to the expiry date on his rulebooks he would lose face and the rest of the round would have gone down the drain. On the other hand I couldn't disregard the valid rules just for the sake of harmony. I decided – how could I do otherwise – for the Rules. Looking awkwardly into the sand I began, "On 1/1/2000 we were given new rules."

Our friend Gardener suddenly went pale. "But these new rules don't apply to Switzerland though," he gasped at once, trying to save a sinking ship. As I was afraid he'd soon start to use Swiss neutrality as an argument I confronted him with the unvarnished truth.

"World-wide. The new Rules came into force worldwide on 1/1/2000."

He failed to reply, so I took a drop in the bunker and we completed the hole in silence.

At the next tee Gardener threw all his rule books in the bin.

"I wouldn't do that if I were you," I remarked, trying to smooth things over, "after all, not everything has been changed. In actual fact only a few alterations have been made..."

I really wanted to cheer him up but it didn't help, it simply wasn't the right time. I don't even think he heard what I said, he suddenly seemed totally indifferent to it all. So we carried on playing in silence and tried as best as we could to avoid any more conflicts about the Rules.

This worked for the next few holes, but then the inevitable happened – Gardener teed-off, his ball brushed a few trees and we were unable to make out where the ball had ended up. He therefore played a provisional ball. We skulked around the group of trees in question looking for the ball – initially without success. Then suddenly Tom discovered it, lying in a fork of a branch way up in a tree. I once saw a similar thing happen to Bernhard Langer on TV but I never thought I'd actually witness it live, however the ball really was stuck in the tree. I couldn't help but laugh out loud although Gardener didn't seem to see the funny side.

"I can now see why your name's Gardener," said Tom, "you obviously specialise in topiary!"

Gardener wasn't exactly receptive to this quip either and merely commented dryly, "I'm not even allowed to play the provisional ball, or has this changed as well?"

"No, no, you're absolutely right, if the ball up there really is yours, you'll have to abandon the provisional ball."

Rule 27-2.c. When Provisional Ball to be Abandoned

If the original ball is neither lost nor out of bounds, the player shall abandon the provisional ball and continue play with the original ball. [...]

"You can play the ball where it lies or declare it unplayable," I remarked, looking up at the tree.

Although my comment did correspond to the Rules it was a bit irrational, as playing the ball where it was lying was obviously out of the question in this case.

Luckily Gardener took no notice and announced without hesitation, "I'll declare it unplayable."

I cleared my throat once more. "But we first have to make sure that it really *is* your ball."

"What do you mean by that? Of course it's my ball, we saw it get caught in the tree, and it's not on the ground anywhere so it must be the one up there."

His argument failed to convince me. "What were you playing with?" I inquired.

"Titleist 1," he replied, impatiently.

I peered intently into the top of the tree but with the best will in the world I couldn't tell whether that particular ball was a Titleist or not.

"As you can't unequivocally identify it as your own, it's classed as lost after all. In this case it means you can continue playing your provisional ball – with a penalty stroke, of course."

Definition "Lost Ball"

A ball is "lost" if:

a. It is not found or identified as his by the player within five minutes

[...]

Rule 27-2.b. When Provisional Ball Becomes Ball in Play
[...]
If the original ball is lost outside a water hazard or is out of bounds,
the provisional ball becomes the ball in play, under penalty of
stroke and distance [...]

Unfortunately he'd already picked up his provisional
ball.

"Great, first you say I can't play with the provisional
ball and after I've picked it up it suddenly appears
that I could have played it after all." He was seething
and I did have a bit of a guilty conscience.

"Then we'll have to find a way to identify it after
all," I decided, "we'll have to get it down."

"Oh yeah," he retorted, "and when I've shaken the
ball down, you'll no doubt tell me that I've moved it
and I'll have to put it back in the tree and incur a
penalty stroke."

There was a lot to be said for this idea.

Rule 18. Ball at Rest Moved
18-2. By Player, Partner, Caddie or Equipment
a. General
When a player's ball is in play, if:
(i) the player, his partner or either of their caddies lifts or moves it
    [...] or causes it to move [...]
the player shall incur a penalty stroke. The ball shall be replaced
[...]

"You're right, this does present a bit of a problem," I conceded, "but don't worry, the Rules have made provision for this situation. If you say in advance that you want to declare the ball unplayable – if it does turn out to be yours – moving it will not be penalised in this particular case."

Decision 18-2a/27 Ball Dislodged from Tree; Circumstances in Which Player Not Penalized

Q. A player whose ball is lodged high in a tree wishes to dislodge it by shaking the tree or throwing a club so that he can identify it and proceed under the unplayable ball Rule. Is this permissible?

A. Yes. The player should state his intention before taking such action to avoid any question being raised as to whether a penalty would be incurred under Rule 18-2a.

He looked at me suspiciously but then I appeared to have convinced him.

"Alright then, I'll declare the ball unplayable. Let's get it down."

We all stood around, perplexed. The tree trunk was so thick that shaking it down didn't come into question, so Gardener pulled his putter out of his bag with resolve, took aim, threw it with all his might into the tree and actually managed to hit the ball. The ball dropped, I picked it up and shouted exultantly, "You were right, a Titleist 1."

But Gardener wasn't joining in the celebrations. He

was still looking intently into the top of the tree, where his putter was now hanging. His face was bright red and saliva had begun to appear in the corner of his mouth. He was fuming and the effort of trying not to burst out laughing brought tears to my eyes too. He then threw one of his woods after it, and to our surprise the clubs came down – both of them.

I was extremely relieved, as I would have felt some-how responsible. But when Gardener took possession of his clubs again we could see that the episode had left its mark – the putter had bent so much on impact that the shaft was now almost at right-angles. With his new piece of equipment in his hand he turned to me and said, "What shall we do now then?"

I tried to keep a straight face. "You're not allowed to replace the club because it wasn't damaged in the normal course of play."

Decision 4-3/1 Meaning of Damage Sustained in "Normal Course of Play"

Q. What is meant by the term "normal course of play" in Rule 4-3a?

A. A club is considered damaged in the "normal course of play" when an action related to making a stroke, a practice swing or a practice stroke results in the club being damaged. [...] Examples of actions which are not covered by the term "normal course of play" include removing or replacing a club in the bag, using a club to search for or retrieve a ball [...]

"Then it looks like I'll have to adopt a new putting style," he muttered and made a few practise swings, which even made him laugh.

"No, you're not allowed to do that either," I added. Gardener could only stand and stare.

"As the shaft is no longer straight your putter doesn't conform to the Rules."

Rule 4-1. Form and Make of Clubs
a. General

The player's clubs shall conform with this Rule and the provisions, specifications and interpretations set forth in Appendix II.

Appendix II: Design of Clubs
2. Shaft
a. Straightness

The shaft shall be straight from the top of the grip to a point not more than 5 inches (127mm) above the sole [...]

"And as the damage didn't occur during the normal course of play you cannot use it in its present form."

Rule 4-3. Damaged Clubs: Repair and Replacement
b. Damage Other Than in Normal Course of Play

If, during a stipulated round, a player's club is damaged other than in the normal course of play rendering it non-conforming or changing its playing characteristics, the club shall not subsequently be used or replaced during the round.

I was beginning to get the feeling that my incessant lecturing on the Rules was overstepping the mark. I wanted to make amends and therefore concluded with the remark, "You'd be better to putt for the rest of the round with your driver, its got the flattest face."

That did it. Now I'd landed myself in a mess. I'd given him unsolicited advice and had thereby earned myself two penalty strokes.

Definition "Advice"

"Advice" is any counsel or suggestion which could influence a player in determining his play, the choice of a club or the method of making a stroke.

Rule 8-1. Advice

During a stipulated round, a player shall not give advice to anyone in the competition [...]

PENALTY FOR BREACH OF RULE: [...] Stroke play — Two strokes.

As neither Gardener nor Tom noticed the infringement it was my responsibility to draw their attention to it. I did it reluctantly. The effect was incredible – Gardener's face lit up to such an extent that I got the impression he couldn't wait to carry on the game. For him it was obviously a gift from heaven that I'd also come away from the whole mess with egg on my face. We eventually carried on the game with Gardener in the best of moods.

After nine holes we had a short break and for the first time we warily engaged in conversation and by the 18th hole Gardener and I were on friendly terms. After he'd bought himself a new putter in the Pro Shop we treated ourselves to a lengthy drink in the clubhouse, where we even managed to laugh about our shared adventure. We also arranged to play together again – but the next round was to be a friendly!

The Good, the Bad and the Ugly

One of the good things about stroke play is that you're not dependent on anyone or anything (apart from the weather). You don't even have an opponent. At worst you might have a partner, but usually everyone plays for themselves and you're completely left to your own devices. As a result there is neither envy nor rivalry – well, that's what I used to think anyway. But a little while ago I played in a tournament that was completely different. I met my fellow-competitors on the first tee and everything in the world seemed rosy. I could see one of them from a long way off as he stood out from the green landscape remarkably well. He had bright red checked trousers, a red bleached shirt and a fiery red face. Even his driver had a red head. The third player looked very ordinary in comparison – neither short nor tall, neither fat nor thin and if you were to see him on the driving range you wouldn't take a second look. He appeared totally uninteresting and harmless – but he wasn't to be underestimated.

On the first tee he had the honor, which wasn't particularly difficult since the order of play was determined by the order of the draw.

Rule 10. Order of Play
10-2. Stroke Play
a. Teeing Ground
The competitor who shall have the honor at the first teeing ground shall be determined by the order of the draw. [...]

He strutted up to the tee and announced, "I'm playing an Ultra 4!"

He played it ultra badly, into the bushes somewhere – at any rate there was no point in looking for it, and his face turned red too.

"Then I'll just have another go," he growled and bent over to place a new ball on the tee, which was still in the ground.

"Let your fellow-competitors tee-off first," requested the starter.

Rule 10. Order of Play
10-3. Provisional Ball or Second Ball from Teeing Ground

If a player plays a provisional ball or a second ball from a teeing ground, he shall do so after his [...] fellow-competitor has played his first stroke. [...]

Reluctantly and with an irritated expression he picked up his tee and cleared the teeing ground. It was obvious how onerous it was to him that we were playing as well. After sullenly watching us hit our balls as straight as arrows down onto the fairway he prepared to make his second drive, this time hitting it tolerably well. Despite this his face remained red for a good while longer.

It turned out to be a very difficult game as the course was completely soaked after continuous rainfall.

Puddles had formed in a number of places and some of the bunkers were completely under water. My red-clothed friend chose exactly one such bunker to play his ball into. He looked at me with wide eyes.

"If a ball lies in a puddle you can take a drop, can't you – for puddles in bunkers too?" I nodded. "So you can drop the ball on a dry spot, not nearer the hole, but still in the same bunker," he continued. He'd got it more or less right and I nodded again. "But what do I do when the entire bunker is full of water?"

"Yeah, that really is bad luck," I began, "if you can't find a place in the bunker where you think you can play the ball there's nothing else you can do but take a drop outside the bunker, behind it, on an extension of the line from the hole to the ball. But you'll incur a penalty stroke for that."

Rule 25-1. Abnormal Ground Conditions
b. Relief

[...]

(ii) In a Bunker: If the ball is in a bunker, the player shall lift and drop the ball [...]

(b) Under penalty of one stroke, outside the bunker keeping the point where the ball lay directly between the hole and the spot on which the ball is dropped, with no limit to how far behind the bunker the ball may be dropped [...]

The player has two options open to him in the case of interference due to abnormal ground conditions in the bunker:

a. The ball may be dropped *without penalty* in the bunker within 1 club-length of the nearest point, where the maximum available relief is afforded, not nearer to the hole.

b. The ball can also be dropped outside the bunker – but with a *1 stroke penalty*.

    This comes into consideration especially when the nearest point of relief cannot be found within the bunker i.e. when the entire bunker is temporarily filled with water.

"Penalty stroke?" he retorted, "I thought relief from puddles is always free from penalties."

"Normally, yes," I tried to explain, "but in this particular case it incurs a penalty stroke as you're allowed to drop outside the bunker."

"But that's not fair," he said, refusing to accept it, "I'd really like to take a drop in the bunker, but it's full of water ... that's not my fault."

"Yes it is," chipped in Mr. Inconspicuous. We listened attentively. "Of course it's your fault. Or wasn't it you who played the ball into the swamp after all?" he barked. As neither of us could think of anything to say he concluded smugly, "Well there you are then," and turned away.

We were completely dumbfounded. My fellow-competitor took a drop and a penalty stroke and we strode on ahead in silence. At the ninth hole the redhead was putting for a birdie when his ball stopped still, right on the edge of the hole. He ran to the hole, raced round it and finally stopped so that his shadow fell exactly over the hole. He then waited and I started to count under my breath. After seven seconds the ball dropped and I congratulated him on his birdie.

Rule 16-2. Ball Overhanging Hole

When any part of the ball overhangs the lip of the hole, the player is allowed enough time to reach the hole without unreasonable delay and an additional ten seconds [...]

The uproar from our fellow-competitor was immense. "I saw you letting your shadow fall on the ball. You can't pull one over on an old hand like me!" he thundered. As the redhead just looked at him blankly he went on, "Everyone knows that grass cools down and straightens up when it's in the shade. It's obvious that the ball will fall into the hole then." He'd turned to me, probably hoping that I'd corroborate this, but as I'd never heard anything like it before and also doubted that the grass could cool down enough in just seven seconds, I made no response. "Tell him, tell him," he urged. I found his theory so ridiculous that I started to get sarcastic.

"Oh yes," I began, "a bit of dew probably formed on the grass and..."

This was obviously not what he'd wanted to hear as he stamped away in a temper in the direction of the clubhouse.

"I'll show you," he shouted.

As we reached the clubhouse he'd already found himself a decisions book.

"There's a decision on it," he announced, "just a moment."

We were very interested to see what he would come up with, but when he did eventually find the decision he no longer wanted to read it out to us – it wasn't what he'd expected.

Decision 16-2/3 Casting Shadow on Ball Overhanging Hole

Q. A player's ball came to rest overhanging the edge of the hole. The player walked up to the hole and cast his shadow on the ball, believing that this would cause the grass to wilt and his ball to fall into the hole. Was the player in breach of Rule 1-2 (Exerting Influence on Ball) when he cast his shadow on the ball?

A. No.

"So, does the grass straighten up or does it wilt?" I taunted.

He took no notice and just snapped, "The birdie may have conformed to the Rules but it certainly wasn't sportsmanlike!"

He obviously begrudged him his good result and I asked myself who it really was that was being unsportsmanlike. After all, the shadow could have caused the ball to freeze onto the grass and then it would never have fallen in! I kept this thought to myself.

After the redhead had teed-off on the 10th hole he casually asked the bad guy, "Do you breathe in or out when you make a shot?"

"What?" he asked with dismay.

"Oh, nothing, forget it."

We never did find out whether he breathed in or out, but one thing we could say for sure – he didn't once have the honor on the back nine!

Forty Winks

I'm sure you've already noticed that there are many different types of golf players. These differences are particularly noticeable in the way various players address the ball – 'address' being an appropriate name for this ritual. Each player has a totally unique style and their own method, one could even say eccentricity, for approaching the ball. Some players are casually nonchalant, seem totally unfocused and even carry on a conversation while taking their back swing. Others, on the other hand, need absolute silence to prepare their shot. The slightest sound – even if it's only the twittering of birds – ruffles them and provokes them to break off their ritual. Accordingly, the round always takes that bit longer with this type of person. The remarkable thing is, that despite their intense concentration, they don't play any better.

The worst type are those players who position them-selves at the ball, wiggle their bottom three times, then pump the club grip, waggle the club, look at the flag, look at the ball, wiggle their bottom, waggle the club, bottom, flag, ball, club etc., etc. until they eventually find their final position. And this position is apparently extremely comfortable as the player then falls into a sort of semi-conscious state and abso-lutely nothing else happens for a relatively long period of time.

I recently had just such a sleepyhead as a fellow-player. As I had been given prior warning – he is commonly known as "The Professor" – I timed him on the first tee. After he had taken 40 seconds to find exactly the right stance he froze for another 30 seconds in his address position. A whole 30 seconds! If they ever staged a golf-sleeping Masters in Augusta he would definitely win the Green Nightshirt.

I was on the verge of saying, "Go on then, play, you can go to sleep at home. It's much more comfortable there and you can drool onto your pillow without being disturbed." But it was only the first tee so I restrained myself. As nothing happened I eventually took the trouble to bend over and look into my fellow-player's face from below, and to my surprise he wasn't asleep at all. He was bent over the ball which he was supposed to be hitting and, despite the deadly serious expression on his face, something seemed to stop him taking a shot. He was staring at the ball with a furrowed brow (until he noticed me and then he started to stare at me instead).

Have you any idea what goes on in the head of this type of player at a moment like this? Please, not left into the water, please, not right into the bushes, please, not into the bunker, please, no cramp like last time, please... But perhaps these people aren't thinking about golf at all. Did I turn the tap off?

Did I shut the garage door? Or could it be that they are plagued by a guilty conscience? My wife is expecting, I hope I'll get back in time. Did I even remember to tell her where I was going?

Whatever the reason, this round was empirical proof that the longer you wait to take a stroke the more calamitous the result. After my interruption my fellow-player set to work refocusing himself. But now he was aware that I was watching him. And I was aware that he was aware that I was watching him. And I was also aware that this would occupy him for 30 seconds again this time. Finally, he made a kind of frantic movement which was meant to have been a stroke and hit the ball so disastrously on the shaft that it flew off at right angles. After a few meters it hit a stone, ricocheted off at full force and flew over our heads straight onto the 18th green.

"Great," I thought to myself, "this'll be the quickest round of my whole life after all. He'll hole the ball, play a round of 70 under par and I'll be rid of him." But there was no chance of this. The Professor glared at me, totally infuriated. From his point of view I was completely to blame. But it wasn't my fault at all. O.K., I'd put him off the first time but then I'd given him a great deal of time to focus himself again. To my surprise he teed-up again without giving it a second thought, leaving me to ask myself why he wasn't going to play his original ball. Of course, every player has the option of abandoning his ball and playing another one. This wouldn't be classed as a wrong ball as every player has the fundamental right to put a new ball in play under penalty of stroke and distance.

Decision 27/17 Status of Original Ball If Another Ball Played Under Stroke-and-Distance Procedure

In general, if a player after playing a stroke plays another ball under a stroke-and-distance procedure, the original ball is lost and the other ball is the ball in play under penalty of stroke and distance. [...]

But of course it doesn't particularly make sense to do it, especially when the original ball is neither lost nor lying badly. I therefore saw it as my duty to point out to my fellow-player how unusual his course of action was. But he only replied, "Can you see that road?" He was referring to the approach road which went between the first tee and the 18th green. "It's out of bounds." With this he took up his stance again in front of his ball and started to wiggle.

"Says who?" I asked, interrupting his ritual for a second time, since the road wasn't marked in any way. He looked at me in annoyance, "Local Rule." I proceeded to fish out my scorecard which induced another belligerent comment. "Believe me, I know my home course."

I remained undeterred and read what was on the scorecard.

"The road between holes 1 and 18 is considered out of bounds."

The Professor was already in his sleeping phase and I wasn't really sure whether I should interrupt him again, but I decided that what I had to say could be to his benefit. I cleared my throat and said, "Excuse me..."

He couldn't believe it, "What's the matter now?"

"You're right, the road is out of bounds," I affirmed, "but only the road. Your ball's on the other side of the road and therefore back on the course."

He found this totally implausible. "No, no, that's not right..." he replied. But somehow it appeared that my argument appealed to him after all for he began to think it over. However he nevertheless concluded, "And anyway if this was the case it really isn't the idea behind the Local Rule and it certainly wouldn't make any sense."

He was definitely right there; a hooked ball which lands on the road is out, while an even greater hook is supposed to be in play! But that's the way it goes sometimes and Rules don't necessarily have to make sense. Therefore I explained the point in more detail.

Decision 27/20 Public Road Defined as Out of Bounds Divides Course; Status of Ball Crossing Road

Q. A public road defined as out of bounds divides a course. A ball crosses the road and comes to rest on the part of the course on the other side of the road. Is the ball out of bounds?

A. No. Since the ball lies on the course, it is in bounds unless a Local Rule provides otherwise. [...]

I concluded with the remark, "So you can play with the original ball. After all it's lying well and you'd save a penalty stroke." As soon as I'd said this I flinched. Had I just given him advice? Luckily not, as guidance on the Rules is not penalised.

Definition "Advice"

[...]

Information on the Rules or on matters of public information, such as the position of hazards or the flagstick on the putting green, is not advice.

My suggestion convinced him and he took his ball off the tee, which was absolutely no problem because the teed ball was not yet in play, and as long as a ball is not in play a player may change his mind.

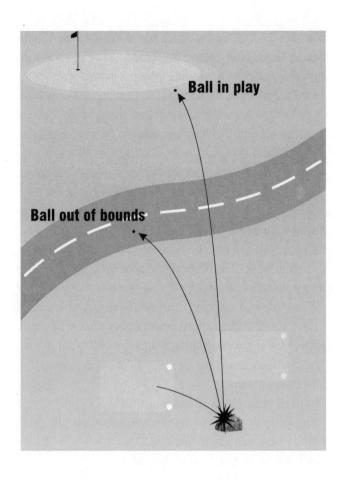

Ball in play

Ball out of bounds

If a road is designated out of bounds and the Local Rules have no stipulations to the contrary only the road itself is out of bounds. A ball which crosses this road and comes to rest on the other side is back on the course and is not classed as out of bounds.

Decision 27-1/1 Original Ball Found Within Five-Minute Search Period After Another Ball Teed

Q. A player plays from the teeing ground, searches briefly for his ball and then goes back and tees another ball. Before he plays the teed ball, and within the five-minute search period, the original ball is found. May the player abandon the teed ball and play the original ball?

A. Yes. The teed ball was not in play since the player had not yet made a stroke at it — see Definition of "Ball in Play."

So we marched to the 18th green where we discovered that the ball wasn't on the green after all, but just to the side of it. The Professor picked it up and got ready to take a drop.

"What are you doing?" I asked aghast.

"I'm taking relief. Everyone knows that you can't play from the wrong green."

"But you're not on the green, you're on the fringe," I corrected him.

He then realised he'd made a mistake.

"But I'd have to stand on the green to play the ball. I must be given relief for this."

Unfortunately this is not the case.

Rule 25-3. Wrong Putting Green
a. Interference

Interference by a wrong putting green occurs when a ball is on the wrong putting green. Interference to a player's stance [...] is not, of itself, interference under this Rule.

"What should I do then – stand on the green, play the ball as it lies and make a divot in the fringe?"

I had to admit that this wasn't exactly a satisfactory solution, but unfortunately the Rules don't make provision for protecting the fringe, and as we were playing a tournament he had no other choice.

"Alright then," he puffed, suddenly no longer seeming to care in the least and he placed his ball back on the fringe of the green. "Then I suppose I'll get a penalty stroke because I moved my ball while it was at rest."

Rule 18. Ball at Rest Moved

18-2. By Player, Partner, Caddie or Equipment

a. General

When a player's ball is in play, if:

(i) the player, his partner or either of their caddies lifts or moves it, touches it purposely [...]

the player shall incur a penalty stroke. The ball shall be replaced [...]

"Yes, that's right," I muttered apologetically, as I really did feel sorry for him. After my attempts to help him he was in a worse position than if he had played another ball from the tee in the first place. And the worst thing was that he had the whole round ahead of him, giving him plenty of time to think about his misfortune on the first hole every time he addressed the ball.

PS: Of course there are people at the other end of the spectrum. In my club, for example, we have Jim, the exact opposite. He practically plays the ball on his way past. It happens so quickly that I usually don't even have time to stand still and be quiet. Sometimes I even have the impression that he's already played a provisional ball while the first one is still in the air...

Year after Year

T he final competition of the season brought it home to me that the year was drawing to an end – it was cold, foggy and my fellow-competitors were wearing boots and gloves. One of them even had a pointy hat on – with Father Christmases on it! I sometimes ask myself what goes on in the head of people who intentionally open themselves up to public ridicule. Probably nothing. Anyway, it used to be considered chic to arrive on the golf course with brightly checked trousers and a comical hat. It was simply the done thing and pointy hats with Santa Clauses on were probably a part of this. As I had the honor I stepped onto the tee with the words, "I'm going to play a Titleist Tour Balata 90, number 3, with a Y on each side," as I'd got into the habit of marking all my balls with waterproof felt tip in order to be able to identify them beyond all doubt, in accordance with a specific recommendation in the Rules.

Rule 6-5. Ball/12-2. Identifying Ball

[...] Each player should put an identification mark on his ball.

My fellow-competitor just muttered, "Maxfli 1."
He obviously didn't consider it necessary to identify his ball more clearly. But as the above passage was only a recommendation ("should"), and involved no obligation on the part of the player ("shall"), nothing could be said against it.

The man with the pointy hat announced, "I'm playing a Molitor." I'd often wondered who played with these balls – for my part I always leave these plastic globes exactly where I find them – but now I also knew what Molitor players looked like. They went together perfectly. "I'm playing a Molitor," he repeated and suddenly, after taking a deep breath he added, "a Molitor 4 with a Santa on top and underneath it it says Merry Christmas." More Santa Clauses – I stared at him in disbelief.

"But it's only October..." I pointed out.

"Yes, I know," he replied, "but last Christmas my mother-in-law gave me 10 dozen of these balls and I really want to use them all up before the end of the year." He then added apologetically, "I got the hat from her as well."

It was now perfectly clear – what we golfers have to put up with! For an entire year you're told that golf isn't a real sport and at the end of the year everyone suddenly thinks that it's great that you're a golfer, because there's nothing easier than buying a golfer a Christmas present – the choice is overwhelming. Soap shaped as golf balls, cuff links in the form of tees, plates, cups, ties and God knows what, all with cute little golfers printed on them – bad taste knows no bounds. A golf ball is simply stuck onto each and every daily article and bingo! you've got an 'exclusive golfing gift'.

I recently had guests for dinner and although I had explicitly and prudently said that they weren't to bring anything with them, one of them brought a gift anyway. He must have thought he was being very clever when he chose the little present, a candle in the form of a golf ball on a tee. Terrific! I was so pleased. But he seemed very surprised that I lit the candle straight away. He must have thought I'd put the thing on display for a few years to collect dust. He almost seemed shocked. But what he doesn't know is that I also let it burn after he and the other guests were long gone. To tell you the truth I left it to burn the whole night and the next day I threw its wretched remains straight into the bin.

I'd actually got off lightly as there are also presents which cannot be used up so quickly, if at all. What on earth do you do with them? You daren't throw them away – but you may be able to swap them. A few years ago swapping evenings were all the rage in golf clubs where you could swap your golf presents with other club members at the beginning of the year. But these events no longer take place – after all, what's the point of swapping a toilet lid embossed with a golf ball for a thermos flask in the shape of a golf shoe anyway?!

Be that as it may, I was supposed to be telling you about our round of golf. At one hole my fellow-competitor hit his Maxfli 1 cleanly from the tee into the middle of the fairway and we strolled to the ball, chattering away as we went. As we reached the area where the ball had landed another player was already there – he smiled at us abashed. He'd hit his ball onto our side from another fairway and his ball was now lying about 1 foot from my fellow-competitor's ball.

"You play first," he suggested calmly. It soon became apparent that he'd also played a Maxfli 1 and couldn't tell which ball belonged to him. We stared at each other, perplexed. "Just play either one of them," he then suggested charitably.

"Hang on a moment," I chipped in, "you can't do that. You have to identify your ball beyond doubt, otherwise it's considered lost."

Definition "Lost Ball"

A ball is "lost" if:

a. It is not [...] identified as his by the player within five minutes [...]

"Yes, I know, but the balls have almost exactly the same lie, so it doesn't make any difference who plays which ball." He glanced at me and as my expression didn't alter he then added, "You really do take the Rules very seriously, don't you?"

"I don't take them *very* seriously," I retorted and explained to him that rules are rules and can only be taken seriously. "You can only play *in accordance with the Rules* or *not* in accordance with the Rules. There's nothing in between. In competitions we play in accordance with the Rules, otherwise it plain and simply wouldn't be golf."

"Yeah, I have to admit you're right whether I like it or not," my fellow-competitor whose ball was involved agreed at last. He picked up one of the balls, fished a felt-tip out of his golf bag and scrawled something on his ball.

"I'll go back then and hit another one – Maxfli 1 with a skull and crossbones on it."

This of course caused the other player a great deal of embarrassment and he apologised a thousand times over. But it wasn't his fault; it was just bad luck, although either player could have prevented it. Then he too slowly made his way back.

After our fellow-competitor had teed-off again, I began to look for the other player's ball. I reluctantly followed him into the high rough and I was suddenly very glad that I had been immunised against ticks. After wandering through the undergrowth for about three minutes he suddenly shouted exultantly, "I've got it!" He came crawling out of the bushes and made for his golf trolley. As he passed he explained, "The ball is lying under a thick tuft of grass, but I can bend it to the side."

"Why?" I asked in amazement.

"Because otherwise I wouldn't be able to see the ball from above. How can you play a ball when you can't even see it?"

"It may be a bit of a pain," I admitted, "but the Rules don't expressly entitle you to see the ball, quite the reverse."

Rule 12-1. Searching for Ball; Seeing Ball

[...]

A player is not necessarily entitled to see his ball when playing a stroke.

"You've got to play it where it lies."

He couldn't believe his ears. He snatched a club from his bag and stamped sullenly back towards the ball. As he disappeared back into the bushes I heard him shout in desperation, "Now I've lost it again!"

So the search started from the beginning again, but not from the very beginning of course because we'd already used up three of the five minutes search time.

Decision 27/3 Time Permitted for Search When Lost Ball Found and Then Lost Again

Q. A player finds his ball in high rough after a two-minute search, leaves the area to get a club and, when he returns, is unable to find the ball. Is he allowed three minutes or five minutes to find his ball?

A. Three minutes.

In the remaining two minutes we failed to locate the ball again and I gave a sound piece of advice.

"Next time you'd better leave your hat by the ball so that you can find it again."

The hat was obviously the wrong thing to mention as he tore it from his head and threw it in such a wide curve through the air that I didn't even see it land.

"Unfortunately I lost the damned hat on the way round, *didn't I?* And I don't want to hear it mentioned again!"

I suddenly thought that this was a pity, it wasn't as bad as all that. But I'm sure he'd soon be given another one, perhaps at Easter – covered in cute little bunnies.

The Gamblers

I once had a boss whose wife couldn't play golf. Therefore, or perhaps for other reasons as well, he burst into my office one morning and asked me if I wanted to go to Spain with him for the week-end to play in a tournament. As I didn't have anything more futile to do, I agreed.

It was a two-day tournament with different formats each day; Better-Ball (Four-Ball Stroke Play) and Greensomes. On the first day the Better-Ball was on the agenda. In this competition each partner plays his own ball and the best result of the two counts. I filled in our joint scorecard and as we were playing net, i.e. deducting the handicap, it was possible that I would sometimes be recording my boss's (usually) higher number of shots.

Our fellow-competitors were called Peter and Frank and they came from Canada. After we had introduced ourselves my boss couldn't resist adding with a broad grin, "My partner's an official golf referee. He'll give you penalty strokes that you've never even heard of." The lads' jaws dropped and they looked at each other as if considering whether they still wanted to play with us at all. So I immediately tried to relieve the situation.

"Don't believe everything my partner tells you. I don't take it quite that seriously – otherwise I'd never have managed to get down to such a low handicap." I seemed to have convinced them as they nodded to us.

But as they strode onto the tee they nevertheless threw me suspicious glances. They seemed to feel watched and they teed-off accordingly. Peter hit his ball out of bounds and Frank connected so badly that his ball only just managed to hop over the ladies tee. However it lay so close to a tee-marker that he was obstructed by it.

"You can move it to the side," I explained helpfully, "the tee-markers are classed as movable obstructions."

"That's not true," claimed Peter, "they're classed as fixed. It says so somewhere in the Rules."

"Yes," I replied, "but only before the first shot, afterwards they count as movable obstructions."

"I find that hard to believe. Are you sure?" he double-checked.

I was sure.

Decision 11-2/1 Status of Tee-Markers After First Stroke

Q. Under Rule 11-2, tee-markers are deemed to be fixed when playing the first stroke from the teeing ground. Are tee-markers obstructions thereafter?

A. Yes.

But I wasn't at all sure whether Peter had understood the basic idea of the competition. After all, the partners in a team were supposed to support each other and it struck me as odd that he had come out against his partner so vociferously. I agree, if the Rules are unmistakable it is admirable to stand up in defence of the Rules, but in this case I somehow had the impression that he wanted to get one over on him.

It took our fellow-competitors a while to get into the game at all. On the first few holes they seemed hardly capable of getting the ball round the course at all. But on the sixth hole they both reached the green in two, much to their own amazement. Peter's ball lay ten feet from the hole and Frank's was only a little further away. After Frank had failed to hole his putt, Peter still had a good chance of a birdie. Together they set about reading the line. Peter saw immediately that the putt ran from left to right, but Frank disagreed.

"No it doesn't, it'll break from right to left."

This assertion produced a questioning look from my boss as the putt was clearly going to break from left to right – even *he* could see that. He couldn't contain himself and blurted out, "I think Peter's right, the putt really will break from left to right."

I don't know why my boss thought he had to interfere; perhaps he even meant well, but after all this was advice, which everyone knows is against the Rules. I therefore told him to keep quiet. Of course he didn't agree at all and insisted that I quote the rule in question.

"Advice" is any counsel or suggestion which could influence a player in determining his play, the choice of a club or the method of making a stroke.

[...]

Rule 8-1. Advice

During a stipulated round, a player shall not give advice to anyone in the competition except his partner and may ask for advice only from his partner or either of their caddies.

"There you are you see," he said triumphantly, "it clearly states that giving advice to my partner is an exception."

"Yes," I replied, "but that means your team partner – that's me – and not the people going round the course with you."

He thought this was just splitting hairs but we ended the discussion as he'd already picked up his ball. Since he wasn't going to record a score the penalty was not going to have any effect.

In the meantime our fellow-competitors were still conferring.

"Believe me, it's deceptive," Frank insisted.

"You must be joking, just look at it," said Peter, refusing to back down.

"No, no, no."

"Can't you see straight, or what? Anyone can tell how it'll run."

"That's what I'm telling you, from right to left."

The discussion went backwards and forwards for a long time with Frank sticking to his guns. After a long struggle they eventually reached a compromise and agreed that Peter should play the ball straight towards the hole. We kept quiet and had to stand by and watch Peter as he aimed straight at the hole. As was obvious from the start the ball broke immediately away to the right.

"Oh no," he shouted, "I told you!"

But Peter just laughed out loud. "That got you. Ha ha ha!" My boss and I looked at each other in amazement, we were completely baffled.

"Frank," I began, "I think there's something you haven't quite understood, we're playing Four-Ball Better-Ball. You're partners – you're supposed to be playing *with* each other, not *against* each other."

"Yeah, I know," said Frank, dismissing my comment, "but we're playing between ourselves as well as we like betting on the game."

I'd never heard anything so idiotic in my whole life. You couldn't play golf in a more paradoxical way than this, together as partners while at the same time competing against each other.

"And tomorrow?" I asked curiously, "We'll be playing Greensomes. How will you be able to gamble then?" [In Greensomes both players tee off, you choose the best drive and then alternate strokes until the ball is holed.]

"Then we'll bet on the longest drive at each hole," they answered, grinning. That was all right with me, as with these tactics we could at least be sure that they wouldn't win.

We carried on the game in good spirits and our fellow-competitors merrily took money off each other. They played so terribly that Peter ran out of balls on the twelfth hole. I thought I could tell what was going to happen – to really earn some money off his pal, Frank would refuse to give him any balls, and simply let him lose. But nothing could have been further from the truth. To my amazement he generously came to his partner's aid.

Decision 5-1/5 Whether Player May Borrow Balls from Another Player

Q. During a stipulated round, a player runs out of balls. May he borrow one or more balls from another player?

A. Yes. Rule 4-4a prohibits a player from borrowing a club from another player playing on the course but the Rules do not prevent a player from borrowing other items of equipment (balls, towels, gloves, tees, etc.) from another player or an outside agency.

I must admit that while I'm well acquainted with the Rules of Golf, I've still got a lot to learn about the rules on gambling. Three holes later Peter had no balls left again, and unfortunately Frank had also run out by then as well. My partner kindly offered to help, "You can have some balls from me."

"O.K., thanks a lot," said Peter, "we'll give you them back later."

"No, no, that doesn't matter," my boss replied. I was amazed. I'd never known him to give anything away before. But then came the inevitable. "You can buy them off me."

At this point it is important to note that we worked for a large bank which had its own balls with the company logo on. We, of course, got them free and now my boss was trying to *sell* them!

"They're our company balls, so I can let you have them for only 1000 pesetas each," he said charitably. According to my calculations 1000 pesetas were about 5 US dollars – and that for one ball?! Before I had chance to say anything my boss winked at me and indicated that I should keep quiet. I reluctantly held my tongue. Frank started to work it out.

"How many Canadian dollars are 1000 pesetas then?" he asked his partner.

Peter also started to do his sums but the heat had apparently addled his brain as after a while he inquired, "How many pesos?"

My partner immediately took advantage of his un-certainty and coolly explained, "I think it's slightly more than one dollar."

"That's O.K.," said Frank, and Peter even added, "Look here, he's almost giving them away."

They took three packs of 3 balls, as you never know what can happen on the last three holes. My boss had taken almost 50 dollars off them and was obviously pleased with himself. I was horrified and whispered to him that he couldn't do such a thing, but he just said, "They're gamblers, they're used to having money taken off them every now and then." We played on and each time our colleagues lost a ball I was seized by a pang of guilt.

My boss had heard and read such a lot about me that he clearly expected me to penalise our fellow-competitors with several penalty strokes at every hole. As we were already on the 16th hole he seemed somewhat disappointed.

"You've not got long left to mete out penalty strokes," he informed me pointedly. I shrugged my shoulders, why should I penalise them – after all they hadn't done anything wrong. As my boss was saying this he climbed into the bunker where his ball lay, picked up a few small stones and threw them into the nearby wood.

"Hey," I shouted, "they're loose impediments. You can't remove them from the bunker unless the Local Rules specifically allow it – which in this case they don't."

Rule 23. Loose impediments
23-1. Relief
Except when both the loose impediment and the ball lie in or touch the same hazard, any loose impediment may be removed without penalty. [...]

"Two penalty strokes," I concluded.

"What?" he shouted, making wild gestures in the direction of our fellow-competitors with his club. "You should be giving *them* penalty strokes, not me! Have you gone totally out of your mind, we're supposed to be a team!"

"Yes, well?" I replied, "that doesn't protect you from getting penalty strokes. I even give them to myself when I've earned them."

He shook his head; he just couldn't understand how anyone could give their own partner a penalty stroke. He thought it a scandal and in protest he picked up his ball and left me to play the rest of the hole on my own.

Then came the seventeenth, a relatively simple par 3 over a pond where my partner had a stroke.

"An 8 iron for you," I said.

"No, 7 iron, we've got a head wind," he retorted.

"That little bit of wind won't make any difference," I rejoined. Now it was our turn to argue.

"I definitely don't want to be too short with that lake in front of the green," he said.

"You're right, but what good will it do to be too long and land at the back in a bunker when you could have been on the green?"

I should now point out that my boss is headstrong and very stubborn, especially when it comes to golf. Therefore he simply wouldn't be told, especially not by me. The more I pressed him the more likely it was that he would use a different club, just to prove me wrong. I finally gave up and he used a 7 iron to hit his ball into the bunker behind the green.

"There you are, you see, what did I tell you?" I said accusingly.

"The 7 iron was the right choice, I just hit it too well." He was incorrigible.

"Hit it too well?" I nagged, "if you'd hit it too well, it'd be in the hole now, wouldn't it. You didn't hit it well at all!"

Our fellow-competitors separated us.

"You're worse than an old married couple..."

We couldn't let it lie at this but resolved to put our disagreement off until later.

My partner then set up for his bunker shot and I couldn't think of anything better to say than, "Just make sure you don't top it, otherwise it'll end up in the water." So he proceeded to top his ball into the lake, and of course it was entirely my fault. The jibes started all over again. If we'd been playing ice hockey we would definitely have hit each other over the head with our sticks, but it was golf and therefore we made do with a verbal beating. Finally I said, "Forget it. I'll manage on my own," meaning that he should pick his ball up and rely on me getting a par.

"What do you mean forget it, I can take a drop."

"Where do you think you're going to drop it then?" I added bad-temperedly, "In the bunker so that you can top it into the lake again? Or perhaps back in a line almost as far as the tee and we'll all wait here in the meantime?"

Rule 26-1. Ball in Water Hazard

[...]

If a ball is in or is lost in a water hazard (whether the ball lies in water or not), the player may under penalty of one stroke:

a. Play a ball as nearly as possible at the spot from which the original ball was last played (see Rule 20-5);

or

b. Drop a ball behind the water hazard, keeping the point at which the original ball last crossed the margin of the water hazard directly between the hole and the spot on which the ball is dropped, with no limit to how far behind the water hazard the ball may be dropped;

or

c. As additional options available only if the ball last crossed the margin of a lateral water hazard, drop a ball outside the water hazard within two club-lengths of and not nearer the hole than (i) the point where the original ball last crossed the margin of the water hazard or (ii) a point on the opposite margin of the water hazard equidistant from the hole.

[...]

"What for? It's got red stakes so I can take a drop within two club-lengths," he replied. I lost my patience.

"But not nearer the hole, and the way the water hazard is formed here there is no spot within two club-lengths which is not nearer the hole."

"Yes, there is," he said apologetically, "but it's only about an inch wide..."

"Super, one inch in which to drop the ball. You know what, you should just forget it; I'm not going to keep discussing the Rules with you. Just make yourself useful and tend the flag."

Affronted, he grabbed the flag and I shot a bogey out of pure annoyance.

And now for the sting in the tail, I have to admit that my boss was right on this occasion. It must be true when they say that your boss is always right. He really could have taken a drop on the one inch wide strip, and if his ball had rolled into the water it wouldn't have mattered at all. He would simply have had to drop it again. In all probability the ball would then have rolled into the water again and he would have been allowed to place it on the one inch wide strip.

Rule 20-2.c. When to Re-Drop

A dropped ball shall be re-dropped without penalty if it:

(i) rolls into and comes to rest in a hazard;

[...]

If the ball when re-dropped rolls into any position listed above, it shall be placed as near as possible to the spot where it first struck a part of the course when re-dropped.

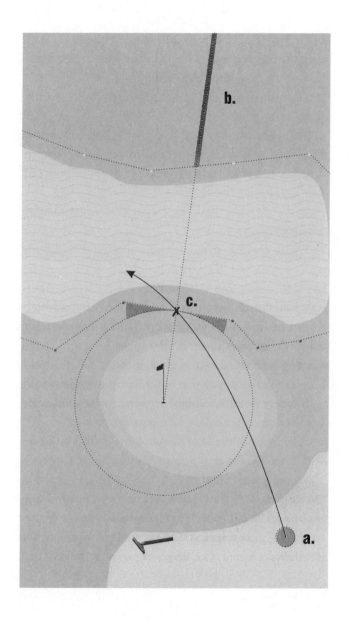

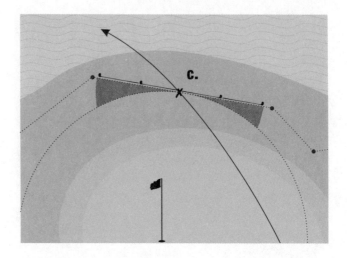

If the ball lands in a lateral water hazard it can be played where it lies, with no penalty. However the player may also take a drop outside the hazard with one penalty stroke

a. at the spot where the last shot was made.

b. on the backward extension of the line from the hole to the spot where the ball last crossed the margin of the water hazard, at any distance behind the water hazard.

c. within two club-lengths of the spot where the ball last crossed the margin of the water hazard. As usual the ball may not be dropped nearer to the hole.

On the example in the illustration there are only narrow strips available for the 3rd option. Nevertheless the ball may be dropped on either of these strips and if it rolls nearer to the hole or back into the water hazard twice, the player may place the ball.

At the end of the tournament we were placed second, one shot off the winner, and my boss reproached me for not having let him take the drop – it was all my fault again. I replied that that wasn't the case at all as he would have had to have holed-out from there, which he wouldn't have managed anyway. In reality it was the two-footer that he missed on the 18th on the last day which had cost us first place. A week later we agreed that I should clear my desk and I went into business on my own.

The Novice

I recently played golf on a brand new golf course and what was special about it was that all the golfers were just as new as the course – they were all beginners. The manager of the club had invited me, and a young man called Alex, who had just taken up golf, also joined our group. As we were being introduced, the manager added the obligatory phrase, "Yves has written a book about golf rules." "Oh yes?" replied the other man in amazement. "Isn't there a book about them already?"

"Yes, of course," I replied, "but the Rules are an extremely complex subject and most people have their difficulties with them. So I've written a new book in which the golf rules are described more clearly with the aid of illustrations."

He was astounded. "I have to admit," he confessed immediately, "I've never really paid much attention to the Rules."

Nor to etiquette either, I thought to myself, looking at his sandals and his cut-off jeans with no belt. But it was almost impossible to tell that he wasn't wearing a belt as his white sloppy shirt almost went down to his knees. I tried to discretely draw his attention to the unsuitability of his attire.

"You've got a super Pro Shop." He looked at me wide-eyed. "Great clothes," I added meaningfully.

"No idea," he answered, "I've never been in."

"I'd have a look round if I were you," I went on, "it really does have super clothes and they've got a sale on at the moment."

"D'you know what," he replied, "I hate buying clothes."

I didn't doubt that for a moment, and as he appeared to be a hopeless case I decided to draw the club manager's attention to the issue when the opportunity arose, perhaps he had more influence over the players. Astonishingly, Alex's first drive flew 200 yards, although sadly it landed on the edge of the rough. As he reached his ball he inquired, "Do I have to play it?"

"What else?" I replied.

"I don't know ... perhaps I could just put it onto the fairway." And just to prove that he did know a little bit about the Rules after all he added hastily, "Not any nearer to the hole of course," and then looked at me in anticipation.

"Forget it," I said, robbing him of any misapprehensions he might have had, "you'll play the ball where it lies."

Rule 13. Ball Played as It Lies
13-1. General
The ball shall be played as it lies, except as otherwise provided in the Rules. [...]

Obviously he usually played to a different set of rules as playing out of the rough appeared to be a whole new ball game to him.

"Can I at least take a practice swing?" he inquired.

"You can ground your club and take as many practice swings as you like. This is only forbidden in hazards."

Rule 13-4. Ball in Hazard

Except as provided in the Rules, before making a stroke at a ball which is in a hazard [...] the player shall not:

[...]

b. Touch the ground in the hazard or water in the water hazard with a club or otherwise [...]

Note: At any time, including at address or in the backward movement for the stroke, the player may touch with a club or otherwise [...] grass, bush, tree or other growing thing.

He missed completely, and as if that wasn't enough he proceeded to miss the ball on his second attempt too. He did manage to hit it the third time round though and the ball hopped back onto the fairway. We finished the hole and Alex announced proudly, "Five."

"Seven," I corrected.

"What?" he shouted indignantly.

But before he could add anything I reminded him, "You've forgotten those two misses in the rough."

Such things have been known to happen. A friend of mine who's a psychologist once explained it to me. Every player does their best to forget their bad shots straight away so that they don't haunt them for the rest of the round and ruin the game. And that's how it should be. So if you really do manage to push these bad experiences to the back of your mind then it's perfectly possible that you'll have forgotten them by the end of the hole. But Alex hadn't forgotten the two misses after all.

"Yes, I did miss twice, that's right," he admitted and added triumphantly, "but I didn't touch the ball."

I looked at him in disbelief, "All the worse."

Now it was Alex's turn to stare in amazement. He couldn't understand what was going on – we seemed to be talking at cross purposes. This prompted me to go into more detail.

"Whether you hit the ball or not doesn't make a bit of difference," I explained, "what does matter is that you made a swing with the *intention* of hitting the ball."

Definition "Stroke"

A "stroke" is the forward movement of the club made with the intention of fairly striking at and moving the ball [...]

"But that's unfair..." he protested. I took no notice. He didn't exactly seem the right person to hold a discussion about fairness or unfairness, or the wisdom or foolishness of the Rules with. Apart from that I couldn't have cared less because we weren't even playing in a competition – he could record what he wanted.

A few holes later the following incident occurred. Alex had teed-off and for once his ball was lying in the middle of the fairway. He then took up his stance in front of his ball in order to make a practice swing. But he did this so close to the ball that his club unfortunately brushed the ball, carrying it forwards at an angle for approximately 20 yards. With a sour expression on his face Alex grabbed his trolley and sauntered away. As the manager and I stayed where we were I called after him, "Actually you really should play the ball again from here." He looked at us inquiringly and I explained, "To play according to the Rules you would have to replace the ball under penalty of one stroke because you moved it."

Rule 18. Ball at Rest Moved

18-2. By Player, Partner, Caddie or Equipment

a. General

When a player's ball is in play, if:

(i) the player, his partner or either of their caddies lifts or moves it [...] or causes it to move [...]

the player shall incur a penalty stroke. The ball shall be replaced [...]

"Yes," he said, half pleadingly, half knowingly, "but I could just *say* that it was a stroke and play it from here."

"No, you can't do that because it wasn't a stroke. A stroke is only a stroke when the player *intends* to hit the ball. But yours was obviously a practice swing, so you can't claim that you'd meant to hit it."

"Hmm..."

He obviously found this all too theoretical and he played from in front anyway. By this point I couldn't have cared less.

The next hole was a par 3. Alex excelled himself and his ball landed on the green at the first attempt. He then putted so close to the hole that I said spontaneously, "I'll give you that one."

So Alex picked up his ball and announced excitedly, "Then that was my first ever birdie!" The manager and I couldn't believe our ears.

"Why birdie?" I inquired, "That was a par."

"But you said you'd given me the last shot." The disappointment and despair in his voice was clear for all to hear.

"Yes I know, but that only means you don't have to play the shot – you still have to count it."

He couldn't get his head round this, "You didn't exactly 'give' it away then, did you?" he growled bad-temperedly. I could understand his disappointment, but you get nothing for free in golf.

And there's something I haven't mentioned yet – we had to look for Alex's ball at practically every hole. Normally I'm only too happy to help my fellow-players look, as long as there's a ray of hope, but it gradually became too much. And when he wanted to look for his ball for 5 minutes in dense clover, even though it was obvious from the start that we would never find it, the manager had had enough too. Alex at least showed some consideration and said, "Go ahead and play on, I'll look for a while."

We played on and at some point we realised that we'd lost our fellow-player. It was the very first time that this had ever happened to me and I wasn't even sad.

Later in the clubhouse I met Alex again and for the sake of politeness I inquired how he had got on.

"Absolutely great," I was told.

Hmm, golf is considerably easier when you don't play by the Rules, I thought to myself. But I soon regretted having asked him, as he proceeded to describe his entire golf round to me.

"You won't believe what happened on the 1st hole. I hit an *enor*mous tee shot, almost 300 yards, but I was terribly unlucky and the ball landed in the rough..."

"Alex," I interrupted, "I was there."

He looked at me wide-eyed. "Oh yes, so you were, but, but... we lost each other at the 8th hole. I'll have to tell you what happened after that..."

He was remorseless. So I had to endure his stories and each time I tried to creep away he pinned me down again and described another hole. And as we finally got through the whole round he actually began on the previous day's round! I had to get away before I blew a fuse.

Why on earth does everyone feel the need to rabbit on about their rounds of golf? Of course, if something spectacular had happened you could understand it – if a ball had got stuck in a tree or a goat had eaten the ball for instance. Or a hole-in-one, at least then you can get drunk at the player's expense while you're listening. But no, most people just ramble on about any old trivial details from their mediocre round of golf. And the worst of it is, the other players actually listen to it, but not because they're interested, oh no, but because then the other person is obliged to listen to their stories in return. Do golfers ever actually have a conversation with each other?

The Cheat

I n our club we've got a cheat – his name is Eddy. Everyone knows he cheats and he probably knows it himself more than anyone else. Or perhaps he doesn't. Whatever, no one's been able to prove it yet. I couldn't judge myself, as I'd never had the pleasure of playing with him. But I had heard the rumors. For instance, my friend Max played with him once and Eddy hit his ball so far into the wood that you couldn't hear so much as a crack as it landed. So Max didn't even bother to go to the wood to help him look for it. Despite this Eddy managed to find his ball anyway – on the edge of the wood, clear shot to the green and with an excellent lie. My friend is convinced that Eddy had dropped a new ball with identical markings, but how could he prove it? Another friend of mine, who also played with Eddy once, watched him hit his ball into a water hazard – he even saw the water splash up. But, wonder of wonders, as he reached the water hazard Eddy was already on the other side – next to his ball. And before my friend had had the chance to lodge a protest Eddy called out, "I've got it, what a piece of luck. It got over." And he was beaming with joy, as if he'd just won the lottery. At any rate, it sounded so plausible that my friend began to doubt what he'd seen. Perhaps the ball really had managed to skid across the water. Even though it seemed highly improbable, he decided not to protest any more.

Anyway, nobody knew for sure. Suffice it to say that Eddy's balls kept turning up under mysterious circumstances, even when they appeared to have been lost forever. Moreover they always had a good lie, which is even more surprising when you consider that the basic principle of golf is to play the ball where it lies – for the very reason that it usually lies badly.

At any rate these wondrous things happened with astounding regularity, sometimes several times in one round. Of course this was bound to have its repercussions. At the weekend we have a list of starting times on which you can enter your name, and whenever Eddy's name appears no-one else's name is written next to it. The only exception is for competitions, when a draw is made for the groupings, and if you're extremely unlucky you have to play with Eddy. For one monthly competition I had drawn the short straw. Eddy and me – an unlikely pairing. I resolved to catch him out at last.

Eddy appeared to be a really nice chap. He introduced himself and tried to make conversation, but I wasn't really listening. My vivid imagination was already picturing his scams. Was he going to throw his ball out of pot bunkers with his bare hands? And would he be smart enough to throw some sand out as well to make it look more realistic? I couldn't wait to see what would happen.

A man called Jim was also playing with us. It was obvious that he'd also heard about the mysterious incidents which Eddy had been involved in, as he watched him like a hawk and interpreted Eddy's every move as an infringement of the Rules. On the second green Eddy missed a six-footer and then finished the hole. After we had all holed out he put his ball back where it had been in order to have another try.

"Ha, ha," shouted Jim, "two penalty strokes for practising on the course."

He was referring to Rule 7-2, which prohibits making practice strokes during the round. However what he hadn't realised was that practising a putt on the last hole played is expressly exempt from the ruling.

Rule 7. Practice
7-2. During Round

A player shall not play a practice stroke either during the play of a hole or between the play of two holes except that, between the play of two holes, the player may practice putting or chipping on or near the putting green of the hole last played [...] provided such practice stroke [...] does not unduly delay play [...]

We sorted out the problem and Jim must have realised that he was being a bit over-sensitive, as he kept his mouth shut after that. I was still curious to see what would happen, but for a time nothing did.

We then reached the 5th hole. It was a par 3 and the green was slightly raised so that you couldn't see the ball land. We all teed-off reasonably well but when we reached the green we could only see the balls Jim and myself had hit, there was no trace of Eddy's. We thought this was odd as Eddy's drive had been the straightest of them all. Perhaps a bit short but we'd all assumed that we'd be able find it without any problems. We looked everywhere but Eddy's ball was nowhere to be seen. He was obviously annoyed because he'd been playing really well up to this point and couldn't understand why his ball suddenly seemed to have disappeared. Just before the five minutes were over Eddy walked round the green one more time. I was watching his every move. With his hands in his trouser pockets he shuffled his foot in the semi-rough. Suddenly he shouted in delight, "I've got it, what a piece of luck. I knew it had to be around here somewhere."

I couldn't believe my ears. The ball had clearly bounced in front of the green and it didn't seem at all likely that it could have rolled over the entire green, especially as the ground was a little on the damp side. I was convinced that he'd dropped another ball so I walked towards him to see for myself. It really was his ball – Maxfli 1, the ball he'd been playing with since the first tee. His ball must have hit a hard spot and then rolled to the back of the green after all. I had to admit to myself that I was probably imagining things and resolved to concentrate on my own game rather than on suspecting Eddy all the time. I even felt a little ashamed of myself.

Eddy chipped onto the green and as no one needed the flag any more I took it out of the hole. And what do you suppose I found? There was already a ball in the hole – a Maxfli 1! It was Eddy's ball, without a shadow of a doubt. He must have made a hole in one without even knowing it and after wrongfully assuming that he had lost his ball, he'd surreptitiously dropped another. An incredible hullabaloo broke out. There was a great deal of shouting and harsh words were said. I'd been right after all. The scales fell from my eyes; that's why he always had his hands in his trouser pockets – so he could surreptitiously drop a ball down his leg through a hole in the pocket. And he'd actually managed to do it without me noticing anything, even though I hadn't let him out of my sight for a second. It must have taken real dexterity to make sure that the ball didn't get caught up in his underpants! I had to admit that he was an out-and-out professional. But what was I to do now? Check his trouser pockets? And what if there wasn't a hole in them after all? Even if there was one I couldn't prove anything. Eddy denied everything of course. It was a coincidence, he claimed, there were probably even more Maxfli 1 balls lying around the course. He argued that you often find a ball that someone else has lost and mistake it for your own. At least he admitted playing the wrong ball and was prepared to record two penalty strokes for it.

Rule 15. Wrong Ball [...]
15-3. Stroke Play

If a competitor plays a stroke or strokes with a wrong ball, he shall incur a penalty of two strokes, unless the only stroke or strokes played with such ball were played when it was in a hazard, in which case no penalty is incurred.

The competitor must correct his mistake by playing the correct ball. [...]

Strokes played by a competitor with a wrong ball do not count in his score.

[...]

Jim was beside himself. He was convinced that Eddy had tried to cheat but he couldn't prove it and he wasn't at all happy to think that Eddy had got away with it with a par. But I had even worse news for him – as Eddy had completed the hole with his hole in one, the fact that he had then played a wrong ball was totally irrelevant.

Decision 1-1/4 Player Discovers Own Ball Is in Hole After Playing Wrong Ball

Q. A player played to a blind green and putted what he thought was his ball. He then discovered that his own ball was in the hole and that the ball he had putted was a wrong ball. What is the ruling?

A. Since the play of the hole was completed when the original ball was holed (Rule 1-1), the player was not in breach of Rule 15 for subsequently playing a wrong ball.

After I had explained this particular rule in detail I concluded with the words, "Then that counts as a hole in one." Jim tried to protest vigorously but his objections were completely drowned out by Eddy's rapturous jubilations. He rejoiced in his triumph without the slightest sign of embarrassment, performed his version of the Highland fling and raved about his very first hole in one. I congratulated him through gritted teeth but Jim didn't utter a word, he was absolutely infuriated. Naturally Eddy didn't step a foot out of line for the rest of the round – he knew better than to tempt fate.

The only possibility now left open to us to make sure that Eddy didn't get away with it scot free was to ring up all our friends and ask them to meet us at the clubhouse in their golfing attire. They all arrived in time and together we almost managed to drink Eddy into financial ruin.

Even though I couldn't prove anything I reported this curious incident to our president. He didn't seem at all surprised and he decided to bring an end to the problem once and for all in his own way. For the next competition he had himself drawn with Eddy in a group of two. But before they teed-off, the president later explained, he took Eddy into his confidence.

"Eddy, do you know why we're playing together today?" Eddy must have been totally flabbergasted, but before he had a chance to reply our president continued, "Everyone says you cheat." Eddy responded to this statement by going so red that the president himself began to feel a little ill at ease. He therefore toned down his allegations a little. "But I don't believe it myself. I've told the others that they couldn't possibly be right – no golfer cheats or it wouldn't be golf any more. That's why I requested to play with you today, so that I can see for myself." Eddy didn't answer. Apparently he didn't talk much for the entire 18 holes, not more than absolutely necessary anyway. So our president didn't find out much about Eddy. But what he could say for certain after the game was that Eddy hadn't cheated once, he hadn't even tried. However he played 30 strokes above his handicap and curiously enough, since then, Eddy hasn't been involved in any more mysterious occurrences.

Peter the Goatherd

P laying golf with my mother is always something special, but on this particular occasion
a rather tall man called Peter played with us
and he turned the game into a real event. Peter was
about the same age as my mother and therefore I
thought they'd have a lot in common. But this didn't
seem to be the case. After a few holes I even had the
feeling that they were getting on each others' nerves.
Peter was annoyed because he hadn't been playing
as well as he wanted to and my mother was getting
more and more fed up with having to search around
for the balls he kept losing all the time. And she had
a point, as Peter smashed away at each ball as if he
wanted to make mincemeat out of it. It was almost
an offence against the game of golf. I don't know
what he hoped to achieve – he probably wanted to
impress my mother – but he couldn't have been further from achieving his aim. After watching balls fly
off in all possible directions like misfiring fireworks
she began to lose her patience. She finally complained
that he shouldn't keep whacking balls all over the
place like that as she'd come to play golf, not to spend
all day looking for them, for goodness' sake! I took
care not to get involved.

Despite this, Peter proceeded to hit his drive into
the water on the next hole and then announced, "I'll
play a provisional ball."

"Just a moment, you can't do that..." I said, putting
an end to his plans.

"Didn't you know that?" said my mother, getting involved as well, "I'd have thought you'd have learned this rule by now, you play into the water so often. It's a horizontal water hazard!"

"A horizontal... a what?" I couldn't help but exclaim, unable to believe what I was hearing.

"Ha, ha," shouted Peter, "you've got no idea but you still have to poke you're nose in, don't you?" The counter attack took my mother totally by surprise. "It's called a *frontal* water hazard. Not horizontal, frontal!" he said, setting her to rights before doubling up with laughter.

I looked cautiously at my mother and it wasn't difficult to tell that she was on the verge of exploding. I tried my hardest to think of something to say that would save the situation.

"It's neither a *horizontal* nor a *frontal* water hazard," I remarked, putting them both in their place, "it's a *lateral* water hazard, which you can tell from the red stakes." They were now both lost for words and I took the opportunity to explain the point of contention in more detail. "There's actually no such thing as a *frontal* water hazard as the Rules only differentiate between *water hazards* and *lateral water hazards*."

Definition "Water Hazard"

A "water hazard" is any sea, lake [...]

Note 1: Water hazards (other than lateral water hazards) should be defined by yellow stakes or lines.

124

"But it is alright to use the term 'frontal' as it's often used to help differentiate between the two types of water hazards. Nevertheless there's no way you can play a provisional ball now as the ball is in the water. A provisional ball is only an option if the original ball ends up *outside* a water hazard where it could be lost or out of bounds."

"If the ball ends up *in* a water hazard the player must proceed in accordance with the Rules for water hazards."

Peter couldn't get his head round this distinction. "But surely you can play a provisional ball and if the first ball turns out to be in the water then you can use the provisional one."

"No, think about it," I explained, "when your ball ends up in the water you have two basic options – either to play the ball where it lies or you can choose to take a drop in accordance with the Rules on water hazards, incurring a penalty stroke, of course." He'd been able to follow me up to that point. "But if you were to hit a provisional ball and then you found your original ball in the water hazard, on the banks, you would have a choice of playing the provisional ball or the ball in the water hazard. And that's not allowed. In golf you're never given the choice between two balls on the course." He looked at me with a furrowed brow and I elaborated further. "The provisional ball is only meant to save time so that the player doesn't have to go back." He agreed with this. "But with water hazards you can take a drop down the course and you don't have to walk back anyway." He nodded. "That means that in this case a provisional ball would be totally superfluous. It only comes into question when the original ball could be lost somewhere, forcing the player to walk back." I wasn't sure whether my mother or Peter could really follow me, but at any rate they seemed to have taken in what I'd said and they now had something to brood over – both of them.

As we reached the green my mother must still have been mentally occupied with the provisional ball because she putted so absent-mindedly that her ball raced straight past the hole and only came to a halt on the fringe, when it thudded into the flagstick.

"Oh dear, there's two penalty strokes for that," I commented.

"Why?" she said, determined not to accept it. "We'd taken the flag out of the hole, hadn't we?"

"Yes, but the location of the flag has got absolutely nothing to do with it. You get two penalty strokes when you putt on the green and hit the flagstick. It's irrelevant whether it's in the hole or not."

Rule 17-3. Ball Striking Flagstick [...]

The player's ball shall not strike:

a. The flagstick when attended, removed or held up by the player [...] or by another person [...]

My mother was incensed. "That's not right."

"Unfortunately it is," I replied, "otherwise everybody would lie the flag down behind the hole, or better still they'd use the flagstick to putt along."

"Even though it wasn't on the green?"

I shrugged my shoulders. She realised that I was right but because she didn't want to give Peter a chance to gloat she audaciously announced, "Alright then, next time I'll be more careful, but for today I won't count the penalty strokes because I wasn't aware of the rule."

'Ignorance is no excuse' was on the tip of my tongue, but I kept quiet because as far as I was concerned she could record what she wanted, after all she was my mother, and in addition to that this was a private round.

The game took its course and Peter carried on hammering balls all around the countryside. But on the 18th tee the moment had arrived – we suddenly heard 'ping'. You know the noise I mean. Both gentle and harsh, with a loveliness beyond description. When you hear it you know for sure that the ball has been hit perfectly – exactly on the sweet spot. And it was true; Peter's ball took off like a rocket and soared elegantly into the air before it returned to the ground again in a gentle curve. It was as if time had stood still for a moment, we were so enchanted by his masterful shot. Peter was overjoyed – it had made his day – and even my mother was impressed. It didn't matter how badly he had played until now, with this shot he'd shown us what golf was really about; hitting the ball as far as possible. Mediocre bogeys, pars saved at the last minute and birdies aided and abetted by chance – these were no longer of any importance to him. His greatest achievement was to have once hit a drive like a real professional, even when it had taken him the whole round and five packs of balls to do it. It was well worth putting up with four hours of ignominy for this one experience.

But the ball had flown too far. As this particular hole had a slight dogleg to the left, and Peter had hit his ball as straight as an arrow, the ball had landed in the rough. This had escaped the notice of both my mother and Peter. They'd both followed the ball in the air but I presume neither of them could see particularly well in the distance anymore and that's why they hadn't noticed. They must have assumed that the ball had a good lie as my mother praised Peter to the skies and he was in the best of spirits. If they had had their glasses on they would have been aware of the impending disaster. And glasses are definitely permitted in the Rules.

Decision 14-3/3 Standard Spectacles and Field Glasses

Neither standard spectacles nor field glasses which have no range-finder attachments are artificial devices within the meaning of the term in Rule 14-3.

Whatever the reason, the fact is that they didn't see it. As they were in such an exuberant mood I decided not to say anything at this point and we made our way down the course.

As we neared the end of the fairway there was not a ball to be seen, just as I had expected. Peter was beginning to feel uneasy and I thought that the time had come to put him in the picture. "I think your ball was too long. It initially landed at the end of the fairway but then it bounced further on." I then added, pointing to the nearby meadow, "I think you'll find it landed in there somewhere."

So Peter marched to the fence which bordered the meadow and looked probingly into the ankle-deep grass. It was so dense that there was no sense in even looking for the ball. Added to that an old billy goat was standing just the other side of the fence and I wasn't convinced that he would tolerate any investigations on his patch. He'd probably view it as an enemy attack and retaliate with appropriate counter-measures. Peter must have realised this as well, as he just stared gloomily over the fence. He'd finally managed a decent shot and now he was going to be punished for it! That was hard to swallow. But he suddenly cheered up and said, "I actually think that my ball stopped just in front of the fence and that goat there ate it up." He seemed totally convinced and added, "Therefore I can put a new ball down without incurring a penalty."

Rule 18. Ball at Rest Moved
18-1. By Outside Agency

If a ball at rest is moved by an outside agency, the player shall incur no penalty and the ball shall be replaced before the player plays another stroke.

[...]

Note 1: If a ball to be replaced under this Rule is not immediately recoverable, another ball may be substituted.

[...]

"Just a moment, it's not as simple as that," I intervened. "How can you know for sure that the goat's eaten your ball and that it's not simply rolled too far."

"You can tell that by just looking at him," he replied instantly.

"Oh yeah," my mother butted in, "and how exactly can you tell?"

"I just know, damn it," he shouted in despair.

In the meantime the billy goat just stood there and stared at us. With his beard he looked like an old Chinese philosopher, despite the fact that his constant chewing gave him a slightly simple-minded appearance. But I also had a strange feeling that he was smirking at us. Perhaps he'd been a mediocre golfer himself in an earlier life and actually had devoured Peter's ball out of pure spite. But anyway, this was all pure speculation and to make the aforementioned rule count we needed facts, or at least a sound basis for the theory.

Decision 18-1/1 Treating Ball as Moved by Outside Agency Rather Than Lost

To treat a ball which cannot be found as moved by an outside agency rather than lost (Rule 27), there must be reasonable evidence to that effect. [...] In the absence of such evidence, the ball must be treated as lost.

I looked at the goat for a long time. To me he didn't seem as though he'd just consumed a hard rubber ball and he didn't look ill in any way, nor was there any rubber between his teeth.

"We need unequivocal proof..." I decided. But Peter didn't want to concede defeat.

"You mean, stupid animal," he screamed at the goat, "give me my ball back this minute!" Then he turned to me with a woebegone expression. "If I was a professional the television cameras would have recorded it all and then I'd have had the evidence."

"If you were a professional," asserted my mother, "then you wouldn't have hit your ball into the undergrowth in the first place..."

I had to admit that she had something there, but it didn't exactly enamour her to our fellow-player. In the end, he gave up on the hole and ended the round with yet another no-score.

But as we sat together in the clubhouse my mother and Peter suddenly began to get on like a house on fire and so we decided to have dinner together. I realised that they were both much pleasanter people when they weren't playing golf. Only once did Peter's temper briefly flare up again – when he asked the head cook in all seriousness if he could serve him the goat from the 18th hole.

Oh, What a Beautiful Morning!

I was in the middle of hauling my equipment out of the car boot when I was taken by surprise by a euphoric, "Hello, and a very good day to you!" I turned around and there he stood in front of me; a well-dressed middle-aged man (whatever that's supposed to mean) with gold-rimmed glasses and his hair neatly combed. I had no idea who he was and fully expected him to say, "Oh, I'm sorry, I thought you were someone else..." but he just repeated the greeting once again.

"Hello, and a very good day to you!"

His voice carried right across the parking lot and he was beaming from ear to ear. But before I could grasp what was going on and make a suitable reply he had already sauntered off towards the clubhouse, whistling merrily. I was somewhat confused. Greeting guest players is, of course, common practise on the golf course, but his over-friendly manner was intriguing. I watched him walk away with a mixture of curiosity and suspicion. It was obvious from his cheerful, bouncing gait that he was on his way to something pleasurable, something that he would really enjoy – golf.

As I was already running late I paid no further attention to him and got back to preparing for the round. I gathered my belongings together and went straight to the pro shop to get my scorecard. I then proceeded to the first tee. One fellow-competitor was already there and after we had introduced ourselves we chatted to the starter while we waited for the third man.

It was him again! I recognised him by his cheerful gait as he approached the tee.

"Cross," he said introducing himself at the top of his voice and with this he shook my hand as if he were trying to shake a ball from a tree. "Beautiful," he announced before I'd had chance to reply and he took a deep breath. "Simply beautiful."

I was somewhat confused and wasn't sure whether Beautiful was his first name and Cross was his surname – Beautiful Cross? But as he enthused about the 'beautiful morning' once again I assumed that that wasn't the case. I didn't say a word. It didn't feel at all like a beautiful morning to me – I was dreading my first shot.

Incidentally, this hadn't always been the case. In days gone by I could arrive at the tee, babble something about the 'beautiful morning' and tee-off like a professional. But then I committed a fatal error. A golf psychologist (whatever that's supposed to be) invited me to a seminar in my capacity as a journalist. He promised me that I would reduce my handicap by at least 5 strokes after the course, which I must admit was a tempting prospect for someone who at the time played off 5. So I attended the seminar, which began with us sitting in a circle and discussing our primeval fears. And it was then that a lady, who until that point had been totally unknown to me, revealed her most intimate golfing dilemma – every time she was on the 1st tee and was due to make her first shot she was suddenly gripped by terrible attacks of diarrhoea! She then proceeded to describe this in vivid detail, even though I hadn't asked her to in any way whatsoever. Anyway since then, every time I have to play my first shot, I can't help but think about this woman and for no apparent reason I start to get all tensed up and this is reflected in the result of my drive – damn the woman!

(In this seminar I also learned of my morbid fear of water hazards, which until then I'd been totally unaware of. So now I stand in front of water hazards in the knowledge that deep down inside I'm afraid, but that there is no need to be afraid, whilst I previously not only didn't realise I was afraid but also didn't feel afraid ... can you follow me? Anyway, one thing's for sure; I didn't reduce my handicap after the course.)

Our tee-off time arrived and I had the honor. To my amazement I hit an excellent drive, it was the best I'd hit for a long time and I pretended to take it for granted as if I hadn't expected anything else. But the truth of it was that I was so relieved that I involuntarily joined in Mr. Cross's joyful chorus.

"It really is a beautiful morning," I whispered to him.

On hearing this Cross was beside himself with joy. He must have thought he'd found a soul mate. He nodded so excitedly that his glasses completely slipped off his nose. We all teed-off well and as we marched down the course Cross enthused about the early-morning dew, the lush meadows and the fragrant blossom. We all completed the hole with pars and showered each other with compliments. The third player also began to join in our hymns of praise, albeit a little belated. He too had a few superlatives up his sleeve.

"Is there anything better on an early weekend morning than being out on the golf course?"

"No," we agreed.

Cross was looking into the distance. "Just look how the countryside looks, veiled in fog, it's so picturesque."

"You don't even need to look that far," I replied, "just look down at your feet." The fairway was still very damp and as the morning sun shone on the grass, myriad drops of dew sparkled in the sunlight.

"Oh, diamonds," cried Cross, obviously enchanted. In this mood we played the next hole with pars and after three holes we were all still even par. We were already the closest of friends, despite the shortness of our acquaintance, and everything in the world seemed rosy – until the inconceivable happened. On the 4th tee Mr. Cross played a snap hook and his ball disappeared into the deep rough. It hit us like a bolt from the blue. The drops of dew, which had seemed like gemstones just a little while before, had changed into thousands of demonic pairs of eyes which pierced us with their menacing stares. Cross looked at us beseechingly and we struggled for words, as we would rather have allowed him a mulligan, the circumstances seemed so unjust. But finally common-sense won the day and I said, "It looks like you'd better hit a provisional ball." Disenchanted, he did as I had suggested and we then started the search. Normally I refuse to help fellow-players when the ball disappears into waist-high grass, first of all because it's unlikely that it'll be found, and secondly, if you ever do manage to find it it's practically im-possible to hit it out again. But in this case I made an exception in order to express my sympathy for Mr. Cross. However after a few steps I was already beginning to regret my decision, as the grass was so wet that my shoes, socks and trousers had soon become soaking wet. I stomped sullenly through the grass and my mood was promptly met by Mr. Cross's reproachful glance. What were soaking wet trousers in comparison to his immeasurable loss? He wasn't going to give up that easily, that was for sure. After five minutes we were still vainly roaming around in the grass so I remarked, "I'm sorry, but the time is up."

Definition "Lost Ball"

A ball is "lost" if:

a. It is not found or identified as his by the player within five minutes after the player's side or his or their caddies have begun to search for it [...]

"What?" shouted Cross, "it's been two minutes at the most."

When it comes to looking for their own balls all players have an extremely generous sense of time. I've often observed this – even in myself. Therefore I've got into the habit of always looking at the clock when we start to search.

"I've been timing it and exactly 5½ minutes have gone by," I retorted.

"Then you should buy yourself a new watch," Cross barked and his eyes glinted in such a manner that a shiver ran down my spine. His earlier amiability had disappeared without a trace.

We couldn't find the ball and at the end of the hole Cross recorded an 8, to his obvious annoyance. On the next tee he smashed the ball so hard that he completely lost both his balance and the ball, and it proceeded to disappear once again into the long grass – this time to the right-hand side. Without waiting for any suggestions from me, he muttered, "Provisional" and, with the same frenzied technique, he shot his provisional ball into exactly the same patch of long grass that its predecessor must have landed in.

140

We walked down the fairway in silence. When we'd reached about half way the other player approached me and asked anxiously, "Do we have to look for 10 minutes as he's got two balls in there – 5 minutes for each one?" He was obviously afraid that Cross would refuse to give up again, but I was able to reassure him.

"If both balls are lost in one and the same place, then the player is only allowed one period of 5 minutes."

Decision 27/4 Time Permitted for Search for Original Ball and Provisional Ball

Q. Is a player allowed five minutes to search for his original ball and five more minutes to search for his provisional ball, or just a total of five minutes?

A. If the two balls are so close together that, in effect, both balls would be searched for simultaneously, a total of five minutes for search is allowed. Otherwise, the player is allowed to search five minutes for each ball.

But the problem didn't arise as I found the ball after only a few seconds.

"What were you playing with?" I inquired.

"What have you found?" came the prompt reply.

"What were you playing with?" I repeated stubbornly. By this time Cross had come over to where I was standing and was trying to gain a look at the ball, but I deftly obstructed his view.

"Titleist," he remarked after a moment's consideration.

"What number?" I asked, delving deeper.

"Erm... three."

"You're just guessing," I cried indignantly.

"No, I'm not."

"Yes, you are!"

I could tell from the look on Cross's face that he was fast losing his patience and that his liking for me had been reduced to a minimum. He bad-temperedly fished something out of his bag and then held a virtually new pack of balls under my nose.

"Look here, I took my ball out of this pack," he declared defiantly, "and it's got 'Titleist' written on it. There's even one of them left." He snatched the last ball out of the pack. "Titleist, number 3 – and as you seem to know all about it, you'll also be aware that each pack contains three lots with the same number. QED!"

I nodded sheepishly and stepped to the side to let him see the ball – it really was a Titleist 3.

Cross was exultant, even though he wasn't exactly chuffed about the position of his ball. While he was still deciding which club to use for his next frenzied shot I suddenly asked, "Did you take both balls out of this pack?" He nodded. "Then we can't possibly know whether this is your original ball or the provisional one," I continued. Cross failed to see the problem. "You played a Titleist 3 and your provisional ball was also a Titleist 3, so how can we tell if this is the first ball or the provisional one?" I explained.

"That's the original one," said Cross with confidence in his voice, and as he noticed my sceptical expression he added, "this ball is considered to be the first because we found it in the first five minutes." I was dumbfounded.

"That rule's new to me..."

"Look, do you want to help me or not?" he bellowed at me.

"Yes, of course I want to help you..." I replied, somewhat intimidated, "I want to help you to play according to the Rules."

This put him in such a rage that I was afraid he was about to murder me. But fortunately the third player diverted Cross's attention by saying, "The way I see it is that you can't tell the two balls apart, therefore according to the Rules you're unable to identify them, and so they're both classed as lost."

I couldn't believe that he was adding more fuel to the fire. Now Cross really was getting cross.

"Hey you, have you gone totally mad? You're trying to finish me off...," he gasped for breath, "they're trying to finish me off."

He had such a glazed expression on his face that I started to feel extremely uneasy. The way in which he was clenching his club also meant no good so I tried to calm him down.

"Don't worry, Cross, the ball's not lost, that wouldn't be right at all, but you'll have to accept that it'll be deemed the provisional one."

Decision 27/11 Provisional Ball Not Distinguishable from Original Ball

A player entitled to play a provisional ball from the tee plays it into the same area as his original ball. The balls have identical markings and the player cannot distinguish between them. Following are various situations and the solutions, which are based on equity (Rule 1-4), when the above circumstances exist:

[...]

Situation 4: One ball is found in bounds and the other ball is lost or found out of bounds.

Solution 4: The ball in bounds must be presumed to be the provisional ball.

"No way, I'm not going to carry on playing on these terms," he raged. "You're just trying to finish me off. All right then, have it your way – finish the round by yourselves." He held out the scorecard but I refused to take it.

"That's out of the question. You've got to finish the round, no matter how badly you're playing." I immediately wished I'd kept my thoughts to myself as even if he had known how lousy he was playing he definitely wouldn't have wanted anyone else to tell him, especially not me. He was beside himself.

"I'm not playing badly at all, who do you think..."

I made one more attempt to calm him down. "I'm sorry I didn't mean it like that..., but after all, rules are rules. And anyway we've got absolutely nothing against you, exactly the opposite. You've just had a spot of really bad luck – it's such a shame after the round started so well."

He was beginning to come round a little, but his resolution remained the same.

"Nothing doing," he replied, "I've got better things to do than to waste time playing such terrible golf. I've had enough, and that's that!" The squabble was beginning to go too far.

"You can't just stop, that's unsportsmanlike and it's a breach of the etiquette."

He looked at me incredulously. "I suppose you've never given up then?"

"No," I replied, "and I never will, not unless there's a thunder storm or the golf committee suspends play."

Rule 6-8. Discontinuance of Play [...]
a. When Permitted
The player shall not discontinue play unless:
(i) the Committee has suspended play;
(ii) he believes there is danger from lightning;
(iii) he is seeking a decision from the Committee on a doubtful or disputed point (see Rules 2-5 and 34-3); or
(iv) there is some other good reason such as sudden illness.
Bad weather is not of itself a good reason for discontinuing play.

"So you'd only give up under those circumstances then?"

"Yes," I replied somewhat rashly, as he then said, "Good, then we'll play on and I'll have the pleasure of watching you finish the round with a broken nose."

With this he started to dance around me with raised fists. This argument and the ominous expression on his face finally convinced me that it was probably better to let him go after all. Thereupon we played on by ourselves and enjoyed the 'beautiful morning', or what was left of it anyway.

I didn't come across Mr. Cross for a long time after that. I later found out that he had been banned from playing until the end of the season, which had given him grounds enough to resign his membership. Apparently he'd then joined a boxing club...

And What
Do You Do?

"And what do you do when you're not playing golf?" This is the question that you're asked sooner or later on every round of golf, but *he* was the only one who ever managed to ask me before I'd even taken my first shot. The first shot, of all times! How could anyone be so insensitive as to broach such a complex topic before the first shot? I looked at him helplessly, what on earth should I say – referee? I haven't mentioned that for a long time. I once said it when I was a newly qualified referee and still tremendously proud of it. The reply I received then was, "This could be fun," – a comment which didn't improve the atmosphere one little bit, quite the reverse. So I don't say referee any more. And apart from that I don't earn a living from it, which is actually the point of the question. But explaining what I do do for a living is so complicated that I often avoid a proper answer and make something up that isn't exactly a lie but isn't the whole truth either. So what was I going to say? I couldn't for the life of me think of anything and I actually wanted to concentrate on my forthcoming tee-shot. I wrangled with my conscience – should I simply tell him the truth?

"I trade in coffee cups, self-adhesive hooks and foldable treadle scooters. I also paint, write books and do the odd article for golf magazines. I'm a partner in an advertising agency and I have my own publishing company. And incidentally, I have a law degree."

How can you explain that to someone? I can hardly explain it to myself. Sometimes I wish I could say something very simple – for example, "Lighthouse keeper. I'm a lighthouse keeper." My companion might possibly ask where, but with this, the topic would be closed and we could get back to the game. But before I could think up something suitable the starter announced, "Mr. Ton-That is a Rules expert." I couldn't believe it. How could he say something so stupid? Ideally I would have strangled him on the spot, but that would have been a breach of etiquette. "Does that mean he's a referee?" was the reply. I sensed a mixture of fear and revulsion in his voice. "No, no," I said, trying to save the situation, "I'm... err... I'm a lawyer."

"What? Lawyer *and* referee?" he cried, "This could be fun."

I didn't say another word. How could anyone ask such a stupid question – and that before the round had even started?

He introduced himself as Gord. His real name was actually Gordon, which I thought sounded better, but he asked me to call him Gord, so I obliged. He also made sure that I knew what *he* did – he was a headhunter, even though he had studied chemistry and before that he'd studied theology for a term – how fascinating! We played as a pair.

Gord's tee shots were all hit with maximum power – usually in the wrong direction, as I was soon to learn, but he always struck the ball with full force. His very first ball landed in the trees. As if he had expected this, he called out with a quavering voice, "For that which I do I allow not. For what I would, that do I not. But what I hate, that do I." He then added, "St. Paul's Letter to the Romans Chapter 7 Verse 15."

I was deeply impressed. St. Paul had played golf? I had to remember that.

Luckily Gord soon found his ball under a fir tree.

"I can move the branches to the side," he said matter-of-factly.

"Absolutely not," I retorted and explained that natural objects could only be removed if they're not fixed. I'd lost Gord completely.

"But surely I can bend one branch behind another one – that wouldn't damage the tree at all."

I explained to him that according to Rule 13 not only breaking a growing object incurs a penalty, but bending and moving one does too.

Rule 13-2. Improving Lie, Area of Intended Stance or Swing, or Line of Play

Except as provided in the Rules, a player shall not improve or allow to be improved:

[...]

the area of his intended stance or swing [...]

by any of the following actions:

moving, bending or breaking anything growing or fixed [...]

"If the Rules don't expressly permit anything else the most sensible thing to do is just to play the ball where it lies. Then it's almost impossible to do anything wrong," I concluded.

"Oh!"

He wasn't exactly happy about this, but he didn't argue. He took up his stance, grumbling as he did so. Despite having a hefty fir branch dangling in the back of his neck he managed to hack his ball out of the rough reasonably well. But as he was about to set up his next shot he complained, "But this isn't my ball!"

He must have played the wrong ball from under the fir tree and therefore we went back into the rough, where the correct ball was indeed lying near to the spot where he had taken his shot.

"I'm sorry Gord but that'll cost you two penalty strokes," I informed him.

Rule 15. Wrong Ball
15-3. Stroke Play

If a competitor plays a stroke or strokes with a wrong ball, he shall incur a penalty of two strokes [...] The competitor must correct his mistake by playing the correct ball. [...] Strokes played by a competitor with a wrong ball do not count in his score.

"What, so many?" he retorted. "If you give me two penalty strokes after each shot, it'll be my all-time record."

This didn't exactly sound full of confidence, but what could I do about it, after all I hadn't drawn up the Rules, and he should have looked a bit more carefully in the first place.

But for some reason he must have taken it personally anyway, as on the second hole I had the distinct impression that he wanted to get his own back on me. My ball lay on the edge of a pond and so near to it that I had to stand in the pond in order to be able to hit the ball. Admittedly it was a bit awkward and was the type of behaviour normally reserved for the professionals, but the ball had a perfect lie. So I took off my shoes, rolled up my trouser legs and cautiously entered the chilly water. But my intrusion into the habitat of mosquitoes, horseflies and other biting insects didn't stay unnoticed for long and I was suddenly attacked by a myriad of buzzing creatures. I tried to defend myself by madly waving my club around, but I was unsuccessful. Eventually I put my club down on the edge of the pond and went in pursuit of the troublemakers with my bare hands.

I suddenly noticed that Gord was grinning all over his face and that he was counting something on his fingers. As he saw my questioning look he announced smugly, "Twelve." He then inflated his chest and repeated with relish, "Twelve penalty strokes." He was smirking from ear to ear. "First of all two penalty strokes as you touched the ground of the water hazard with your club..."

"Nothing doing," I interrupted him, "there's an exception to this."

Rule 13-4. Ball in Hazard

Except as provided in the Rules, before making a stroke at a ball which is in a hazard [...] the player shall not:

[...]

b. Touch the ground in the hazard or water in the water hazard with a club or otherwise [...]

Exceptions:

1. Provided nothing is done which constitutes testing the condition of the hazard or improves the lie of the ball, there is no penalty if the player [...] places his clubs in a hazard.

[...]

"O.K., O.K.," said Gord with a dismissive gesture – I don't even think he'd heard me properly – "I'll give you those two."

But now Gord played his trump card, "You get ten penalty strokes for the five poor little mosquitoes you swatted away, I counted them exactly. That's two penalty strokes for each mosquito." I was flabbergasted and he explained, "They're loose impediments and everyone knows they can't be touched or moved in a hazard."

I was totally aghast. What he had said sounded plausible enough, but I wasn't prepared to accept defeat so easily and I consulted my decisions book where I actually managed to find something to my defence.

"When you repeatedly breach *one and the same* rule, the penalty strokes don't mount up. Instead, the penalty provided for the breach is only given once. In this case, two penalty strokes."

Decision 18-2a/10 [...]

[...] There are a number of Decisions under which a competitor who infringes the same Rule several times prior to a stroke is penalized for only one infringement [...]

Rule 13. Ball Played as It Lies

PENALTY FOR BREACH OF RULE: [...] Stroke play — Two strokes.

Gord was obviously disappointed, but could see that his interpretation of the Rules had been unjust. But then his jaw dropped completely as I also managed to rid myself of the two remaining penalty strokes.

Decision 13-4/16.5 Flying Insect in Water Hazard

Q. A player's ball is in a water hazard. The player is being distracted by an insect (a loose impediment) flying in the hazard. May the player swat away the insect?

A. Although the margin of a water hazard extends vertically upwards such that the insect is in the hazard, the Rules do not contemplate such a case. Thus, in equity (Rule 1-4) the player may swat away the insect whether it be flying or on the player.

He must have realised that he wouldn't get the better of me with his antics, as he didn't bother to try to catch me out with the Rules any more. He just concentrated on his own game and finally ended the round three strokes under his handicap. He was in the best of spirits.

"I'll hand in the cards, you can go along to the bar and order two beers on me."

As opposed to the penalty strokes, the effect of the beer did mount up very well indeed and we had a high-spirited afternoon. But we soon sobered up during the presentation ceremony when Gord was not amongst the leading positions. He wasn't even on the first page of the ranking list, but was awarded last place. We were informed that as he had failed to sign his scorecard he'd been disqualified.

"What sort of people do they employ in the pro shop," Gord bemoaned, "that they would disqualify me? They know very well they can find me in the bar if they need me. They could have brought me the card to sign."

"Unfortunately not," I replied, "the Rules on this are very strict."

Rule 6-6. Scoring in Stroke Play
b. Signing and Returning Card

After completion of the round, the competitor should check his score for each hole [...] He shall ensure that the marker has signed the card, countersign the card himself and return it to the Committee as soon as possible.

PENALTY FOR BREACH OF RULE 6-6b: Disqualification.

c. Alteration of Card

No alteration may be made on a card after the competitor has returned it to the Committee.

"If you've returned it, you've returned it. I know it's hard and a lot of people think that the penalty's unfair, but it's the same rule for all of us."
Gord's disappointment was written all over his face, but he knew that there was no point in discussing it any further. So he returned to the bar, where the rules, he informed me, were much easier to understand. Cheers!

Out of Love for an Ancient Game

A few years ago I went to the Algarve in the autumn to play golf. They have fantastic courses there – wickedly expensive, but the architecture and landscape are outstanding. The players I met on every course were all outstanding too. Outstandingly bad. I played on a variety of courses, but I met the same players on every one. By that I mean the type of player, of course they were totally different people, but they all had something in common – none of them could actually play golf. I soon realised that to all intents and purposes the Algarve was a refuge for the most incompetent golfers in the whole world. People, who at home would hide themselves from view in a secluded corner at the very back of the driving range and would hardly ever venture onto the course, if at all, dared to be seen on the Algarve's golf courses, because there they were among friends. They came from all corners of the world to fire balls in all directions all day and then look for them with gusto. They had finally found a place where they could do this in peace and quiet, without continually being overtaken by ambitious pairings and being regarded with compassionate or even reproachful looks. There was none of this there. Other customs prevailed. It was open season for rookies.

But don't get me wrong, I don't want to criticise these people in the slightest. After all, a player's handicap says nothing about their quality as a human being, and let's face it, that's what it's all about.

On the contrary, they were all wonderful people, without exception. They didn't have the faintest idea about playing golf but we always had a great time. Nowhere else in the whole world had I ever seen as many happy faces on the golf course as I saw there. One day the renowned Royal Golf Course of Vale do Lobo was on my schedule. I had been drawn with a German couple and I didn't expect for a minute that they would be able to play well, and as I actually caught sight of them on the first tee it was obvious that this would be absolutely impossible because of their considerable size. You could tell from a long way off that they were together. My one concern was how they intended to carry their weight around the course within an acceptable period of time. But as it turned out they had their own golf cart because, as they later explained, they lived directly next to the course where everyone has a cart. The carts were extremely practical, and absolutely indispensable when you went shopping. The warmth with which they greeted me and introduced themselves told me that, one way or the other, this would be an entertaining round. They were called Helga and Hubert. Hubert was thrilled that I was playing with them. Actually they were both thrilled, but Hubert most of all. He loved to gamble, but he never had the chance to do this with his wife. So we resolved to play match play for the drinks after the round. I had to give him two strokes per hole.

"If we're taking bets everything's got to be done properly," he said raising his index finger. I wasn't quite sure what he was getting at. "I mean, we've got to play in accordance with the official rules," he added by way of explanation.

As I didn't know any other rules but the official ones anyway, this was all right by me. I nodded. He then added, "I'm afraid I'm not particularly well-versed on the subject, so feel free to tell me if I do anything wrong." He then turned to his wife and said, "We're going to play exactly by the Rules this time. We don't want the young man to complain after the game, when he has to pay for all our drinks, that we didn't go by the book."

They then both laughed so hard that the cart in which they were sitting squeaked as it rocked up and down. I teed off. Hubert and Helga stood with their mouths wide open, as if they'd just seen a UFO – or the Devil himself.

"It looks like you're going to have to put some effort in," said Helga to her husband.

He just nodded and then they both started to laugh heartily again. Hubert tried his hardest. His swing was extraordinary; a mixture between break-dancing and Robocop. Absolutely hilarious. And the best of it was – the ball really did fly. It may never have gone more than 1 foot above the ground, but it definitely flew. And after it had made contact with the ground again it rolled and flew and rolled and flew, then hopped onwards until it finally came to a standstill in the middle of the fairway. As Hubert saw this he exerted himself a little more to produce a stylish finish and looked proudly in the direction of his wife. She returned his gaze and her eyes reflected her deepest admiration. I asked myself why. He'd actually hit an astonishingly good shot – but I only realised this when I saw how he played the other holes.

On the fourth tee Hubert teed his ball up clearly in front of the tee-markers. As I only noticed this as he was already taking his back swing I didn't say anything, because in match play this doesn't create a problem. While in stroke play the shot doesn't count, the player incurs two penalty strokes and has to tee-off again, the Rules are much more lenient in match play.

Rule 11. Teeing Ground
11-4. Playing from Outside Teeing Ground
a. Match Play

If a player, when starting a hole, plays a ball from outside the teeing ground, the opponent may immediately require the player to cancel the stroke so played and play a ball from within the teeing ground, without penalty.

[b. Stroke Play: If a competitor, when starting a hole, plays a ball from outside the teeing ground, he shall incur a penalty of two strokes and shall then play a ball from within the teeing ground.]

As I didn't want to make our game any more complicated than necessary, I said nothing, particularly as Hubert's tee-shot had once again landed a long way from the fairway. Why should I have given him a second chance, after all we were playing for the drinks and I was only three holes ahead.

So we set off in search of the ball. It wasn't at all easy because the grass, which had looked harmless from the tee, turned out to be high rough and I didn't think we'd got much of a chance of ever finding the ball again, unless one of us was to accidentally tread on it – which is what I proceeded to do. I naturally contemplated whether I should stand on the ball until the five minutes were over, or whether I should content myself with simply driving the ball further into the ground with the heel of my shoe. But I overcame my baser instincts and pushed the ball back to its original position.

"Hubert," I called, "I've found your ball, a Top-Flite XXL."

Hubert was highly impressed as he'd given up hope too.

"How did you manage that?"

"I trod on it. Pure luck."

Hubert grinned at me and said, "Thanks a lot, but don't you get rewarded with a penalty stroke for moving my ball? I think there's some sort of special rule for that in match play."

I was amazed that he was even aware that match play had special rules. Nevertheless his knowledge was only fragmentary and therefore I described the rule in question more precisely.

"You're right, in match play you don't only incur a penalty for moving your own ball, you also get one for moving your opponent's ball. However an exception to this is if it happens when you're looking for the ball."

Rule 18. Ball at Rest Moved
18-3. By Opponent [...] in Match Play
a. During Search

If, during search for a player's ball, the ball is moved by an opponent [...] no penalty is incurred and the player shall replace the ball.

[b. Other Than During Search: If, other than during search for a ball, the ball is touched or moved by an opponent [...], the opponent shall incur a penalty stroke. The player shall replace the ball.]

"I thought that'd be the case," smirked Hubert, "otherwise nobody would ever help anyone look for their ball!" and he promptly shook with laughter again.

I was six up after nine holes. So Hubert said he'd pay for the drinks and proposed a new bet; I was now to give him three strokes per hole and we would play for dinner. I accepted and we began our attack on the second nine. Hubert halved several of the following holes and even managed to win one of them.

As we reached the fifteenth green he pointed to a handsome villa behind him, "That's where we live, with a direct view to the sixteenth and the sea." I was both impressed and bewildered at the same time. "The sixteenth..?"

He waved at me dismissively and indicated that I should putt out first, "You'll see it soon enough." And I did see it as we walked up to the next tee.

"The famous sixteenth, par 3," explained Hubert, "the most photographed hole in the world."

He'd never taken a photo of it himself, he added, why should he? And he was right, I did recognise the hole from countless pictures, but it was far more impressive in reality. The sun was already quite low in the sky and its warm rays had lit up the red sandstone cliffs, making them an even deeper red – they were positively glowing. It was breathtaking. But the distance from the tee was also breathtaking – a 200-yard carry over the cliffs.

We both managed to get over them, even if Hubert needed a few more balls than I did. Eventually, both our balls were in the same bunker, right next to each other.

"What now?" asked Hubert.

"I'll play first as my ball is a little further from the hole. But first would you mind marking your ball and picking it up, as it'll interfere with my shot?"

Rule 22. Ball Interfering with or Assisting Play
Any player may:

[...]

b. Have any other ball lifted if he considers that the ball might interfere with his play [...]

"Oh great," grumbled Hubert morosely, "and then I'll have to play my ball in your footmarks?"

"No, of course not," I said reassuring him, "if the lie's changed by my shot we'll restore it exactly as it was."

Rule 20. Lifting, Dropping and Placing [...]
20-3. Placing and Replacing
b. Lie of Ball to be Placed or Replaced Altered
If the original lie of a ball to be placed or replaced has been altered:

[...]

(iii) in a bunker, the original lie shall be recreated as nearly as possible and the ball shall be placed in that lie.

Hubert was relieved, but in the end he lost the hole anyway. By way of compensation the seventeenth was decided in his favour and it was all square as we started on the eighteenth tee.

I was beginning to get genuinely concerned about losing. As although I'd already won the drinks, the meal was still to be decided. And this would surely be the most expensive part of the bet as, if I had judged the couple correctly, they weren't exactly picky eaters. That's why I desperately tried to find a way to inflict a few penalty strokes on Hubert. However he proceeded to make a mess of his tee shot, so that when we reached the green I still had the chance to putt for a birdie and the match, despite the fact that I had had to give him three strokes. Hubert's ball was lying only a little way behind the hole and therefore he went over to mark it.

"You can leave it where it is, it's not bothering me," I called to him.

Hubert was extremely surprised when he heard this and said suspiciously, "If you hit my ball you'll get two penalty strokes though, won't you?"

I grinned. "There is a different rule for match play. In this particular case there's no penalty."

Rule 19. Ball in Motion Deflected or Stopped
19-5. By Another Ball
a. At Rest

If a player's ball in motion after a stroke is deflected or stopped by a ball in play and at rest, the player shall play his ball as it lies. In match play, no penalty is incurred. [In stroke play, there is no penalty unless both balls lay on the putting green prior to the stroke, in which case the player incurs a penalty of two strokes.]

"But I don't *have* to leave it there, do I?" Hubert then asked. "I'm allowed to pick the ball up any time I think that it might assist the other player. That's the rule you were talking about, isn't it?"

Rule 22. Ball Interfering with or Assisting Play
Any player may:
a. Lift his ball if he considers that the ball might assist any other
   player [...]

I had to admit that he was right. So he did know more about this confounded game than I'd thought. Nevertheless I holed my putt and won the match.

As a result Hubert paid for a round of drinks – this he did with the greatest of pleasure. He enthused that it had been the most enjoyable and exciting round of his whole life and he invited me to partake of the meal I'd won at his house, as his wife was the best cook in the whole world. I was delighted, as I didn't doubt it for a minute.

While Helga got to work in the kitchen we enjoyed the last remnants of the day on the veranda. The glittering red sun was sinking behind the sixteenth hole into the sea.

"I know," Hubert suddenly began, "we've both got a terrible swing. After all, we share the same pro." He grinned. "Perhaps it's got something to do with our build. But it doesn't matter. You know, when you start playing golf at our age, you're not very ambitious. We don't play in any competitions – goodness me, no – we just play our round, sometimes it goes well, sometimes not, but we always enjoy ourselves."

I was sure that they enjoyed themselves much more than most other players. All these obsessed golfers, who spend hours and hours on the driving range and try desperately to reduce their handicap in each and every competition. Helga and Hubert didn't face this problem, after all they didn't even have a handicap... And while he was talking I resolved not to take golf so terribly seriously in the future – you don't have to be a master of the game to love it.

Index of Rules